I don't know
much about
wine...

but I know
what I like

I don't know much about wine...

but I know what I like

Simon Woods

MITCHELL BEAZLEY

I don't know much about wine...
but I know what I like

by simon woods

FIrst published in Great Britain in 2003 by Mitchell Beazley, an imprint of Octopus Publishing Group Limited, 2–4 Heron Quays, London E14 4JP.

A CIP catalogue record for this book is available from the British Library.

ISBN: 1 84000 844 X

The author and publishers will be grateful for any information which will assist them in keeping future editions up-to-date. Although all reasonable care has been taken in the preparation of this book, neither the publishers nor the author can accept any liability for any consequences arising from the use thereof, or the information contained therein.

Commissioning Editor Hilary Lumsden
Executive Art Editor Yasia Williams
Illustrator Roman Grey
Managing Editor Emma Rice
Editor Jamie Ambrose
Production Gilbert Francourt

Typeset in Magda and TradeGothic
Printed and bound by Mackays Ltd in the UK

Contents

the start

I don't know much about wine, but I know what I like...

Hmm. Two things. Hate to contradict you, but you probably
know more about wine than you think. You may not know
the natural colour of the hair, age, and favourite chocolate
bar of the impossibly young-looking winemakeress who
produces Château Blotto Grand Cru in that tiny village in
Switzerland that is also renowned for cuckoo clocks
and yodelling (brown, 43, and Toblerone, by the way).
However, you probably do know that:

> **Cabernet Sauvignon** makes red wines.
> **Chardonnay** makes white.
> A brawny **Australian Shiraz** is a better
> accompaniment to a barbecue than a
> bottle of port.
> And you can probably spot your **favourite
> wine** on a shop shelf at forty paces
> without much difficulty – especially if it's
> on special offer.

And then there's the "...but I know what I like" part.
Again, I'm not convinced. Do you like Pacherenc du Vic
Bilh? What about Jerepigo? Or Bomballerina Bianco?
OK, I made that last one up, but the others do exist
(and I'm not trying to be a smart-ass).

There are hundreds of thousands of different wines produced around the world each year, and even the most enthusiastic and dedicated of professional wine tasters (tough job, but, as they say...) can only sample a fraction of them.

It's a struggle to keep on top of every part of the wine world. For normal folk, as in those who don't spend all day spitting into a bucket, it's almost impossible. It's no surprise that many people revert to two or three tried and tested old favourites, or whatever is in the bargain basement that week.

For me, one of the most exciting things about wine is its sheer diversity.

Just as we don't listen to the same music all the time, or wear the same clothes every day (unless you're a college student), or have pizza for every meal (unless you're a college student), so we shouldn't settle for the same tried and tested wines every time we're confronted with a row of bottles. It's time to experiment – to get cocky with the corkscrew. The world of wine has more to offer than Cab and Chard. Some wines are terrific, some are not. The aim of this book is to guide you away from the latter towards the former.

Maybe the title of the book should have been, "I know a little about wine, and I'd like to find out some more." If that's you, then grab a glass and read on...

1 | you are right

2 | just say "no" to chardonnay

3 | if it sounds cheap, it probably tastes cheap

4 | what's so special about that?

5 | it doesn't look very new to me

all about wine part 1

a head start

1 | you are right
if it tastes good to you...

Don't ever let someone tell you that you're a dope for liking a particular wine. It's *your* mouth you're pouring it into – not theirs. If something tastes good to you, then it tastes good, and you are right – period. Just as some people have a sweet tooth, others have a Sauvignon Blanc tongue, or a Merlot cheek.

> If we all **drank the same wine**, just as if we all **sported the same haircut**, the **wine selection** in the store would be much smaller, the **world** would be **less interesting**, and I'd be out of a job.

And equally, if someone gives you a glass of wine expecting you to go into raptures about it and it makes you shudder, then again: you are right.

However, let me just throw this in as a thought. Do you remember *not* liking chips? Everybody likes chips (and if they don't, they're wrong). However, do you remember your first taste of beer? Did you like it? Almost certainly not, but you probably do now. And similarly, think back to when you were eight and a box of chocolates was passed around. Which did one you go for first? For me, it was strawberry cream. And would you go for the same one now? No way, José: point me to the pralines.

> There are parallels with wine. There are some wines we've always liked and always will. There are others that, once upon a time, we couldn't get along with and now suddenly find indispensable.

It's amazing how many individuals who would once have crossed the road to avoid fino sherry have been converted to the cause by a trip to Spain. And, similarly, numerous people who cut their wine teeth on sweet, oaky Chardonnay, or Liebfraumilch, or Mateus Rosé, would run away from them today.

> It's not the wine that's changed; it's your taste-buds or — in wine jargon — your palate. And that shouldn't be a surprise. Remember what you were wearing ten years ago, or what you were watching on TV?

So, yes: you are right, but the way you are right today isn't necessarily the same as the way you were right yesterday, or will be tomorrow.

2 | just say "no" to chardonnay
why you should experiment more

The words "head", "bang", and "brick wall" spring to mind when it comes to wine and my mother. Well-read, theatrical to the point of high camp and a great cook, she has a blind spot where wine is concerned. The line she trots out is,

> "They all taste the same to me."

I resist the temptation to say,

> "And of course you've tried them all,"

and keep shoving different glasses under her finely chiselled nose in the hope that, one day, something will make her sit up and take notice. Not everyone is as set in their ways as Mrs W., but there are still several million people who, in wine terms, really should get out more. When they wander dreamily down the wine aisle, or drop in to their local wine shop, they almost head for, if not the same wine every time, then certainly the same style.

Cheap California Chardonnays, Chilean Merlots, and **Italian Pinot Grigios** can be honest, decent drinks.

But – and let's be honest here – while the labels for Brands X, Y, and Z might be different, the wines often taste like they've come out of the same tank – or vat, in wine-speak; it sounds better, even if it's still a stainless-steel tank the size of Alaska...

If your definition of being adventurous is simply jumping from X to Y to Z, then maybe you can use the "They all taste the same to me" line.

But there are dozens – even hundreds – of alternatives in most stores. And if you don't try them soon, the message you're sending to the shop owner is that more choice is actually a bad thing. A wall of bottles can be daunting, but you don't have to try them all.

```
            All I'm asking for is a
      Chardonnay-free week (or month, if
   you're feeling game) when you bypass
             your preferred bottle and try
                    something different.
```

Otherwise, the range in stock will get smaller and smaller until all that's left are Brands X, Y, and Z. Do you *really* want that on your conscience?

3 | if it sounds cheap, it probably tastes cheap

why not pay just a little bit more?

Okay: let's see how much a bottle of wine costs. The cheapest combination of bottle, cork, capsule (the wraparound thingie at the top), and label is somewhere around 30p/50¢. Then let's fill our bottle with a cheap wine, that costs just 10p/16¢ to produce. Add carton and shipping, and we're up to 70p/$1.23.

The winery settles for a modest profit margin of ten per cent (77p/$1.24). The importer is feeling benevolent, so he's happy with ten per cent, too (85p/$1.36). The retailer's a little more cash-hungry, but settles for a modest twenty per cent (£1.02/$1.64). In the UK, there's then the matter of duty, or import tax, which adds another £1.20/$1.93 a bottle, plus value-added tax (VAT) at 17.5 per cent. (In the USA, of course, you have to factor in import, federal, and state sales taxes – the last one in all its incarnations). Our eventual bottle price is £2.61/ $4.19 – just 10p of which is the cost of wine.

More expensive liquid costs, say, £1.61/$2.58, and our bottle ends up at £5.22/$8.30. Yet while this wine costs more than sixteen times more, the total bottle price has only doubled. The wine may not be sixteen times better, but the quality leap should more than justify the cash hike.

> Duty rates, taxes, and profit margins vary considerably around the world, but remember this simple message: a few more pennies, a lot more wine.

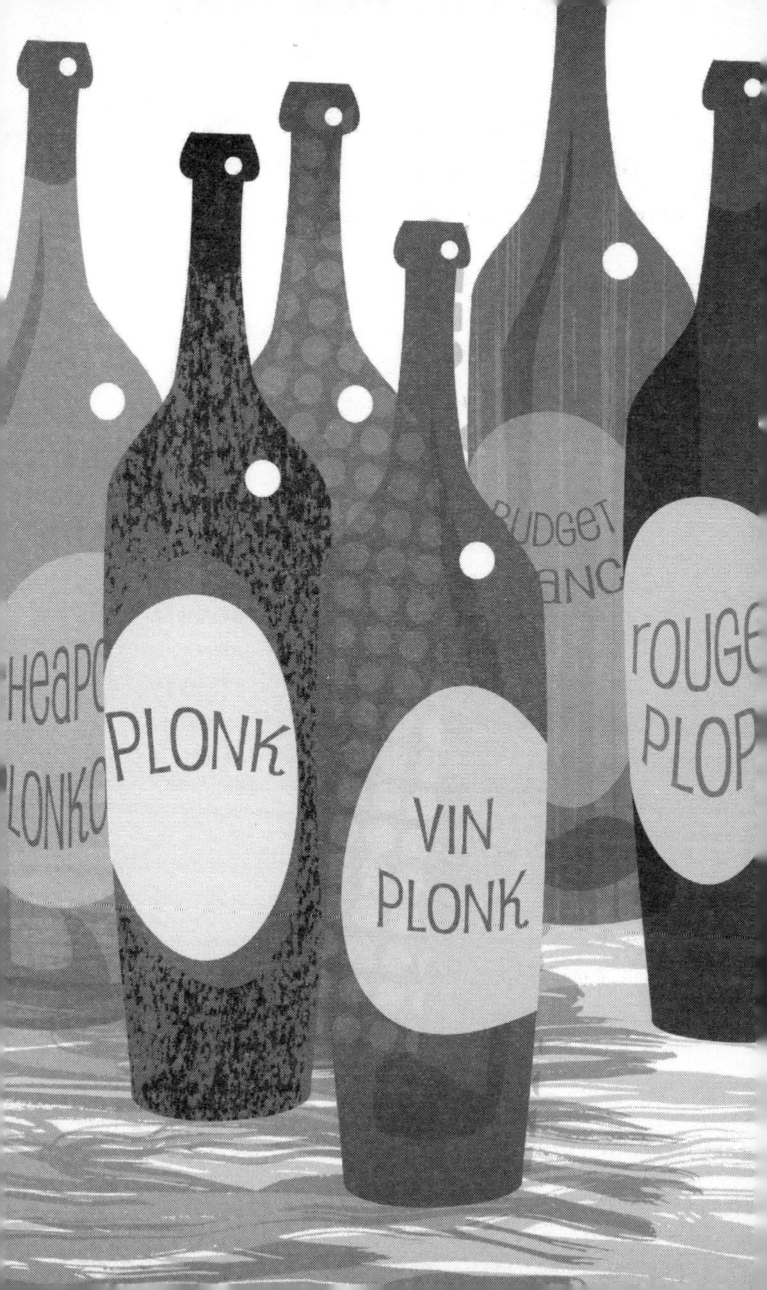
PLONK
VIN
PLONK

4 | what's so special about that?

how special is that special offer?

We all love bargains. There's nothing quite so satisfying
as getting something we really want at a knock-down price.
The same, of course, is true for wine. We resent paying
more than we have to for our booze, and this works out
in two ways, depending upon our outlook. Some people,
for example, will delight in drinking *vin de pays* Merlot from
southern France because it offers the quality and style of
inexpensive red Bordeaux for fewer *centimes*. Others will
head for Store A rather than Store B because their favourite
Sauvignon Blanc is ten per cent cheaper there.

> But when is bargain not a bargain?
> Let's delve into the grubby world
> of wine marketing. It would be nice
> if price and quality always went hand
> in hand – but in wine, they don't.

True, if you look at a company such as Penfolds in
Australia, each step up the price ladder from Rawson's
Retreat (£4.99/$8.01) at the bottom to Grange (£110/$177)
at the top shows a step up in quality.

At that £4.99 price point, there are wines from other
companies that taste better, and there are others that taste
worse. And we wouldn't expect otherwise.

However – and this is where things get murky – many companies around the world now tailor-make their wines for major supermarkets and other big retailers so that they can sell for £4.99 for most of the year, then be promoted at £3.99 or even £2.99 ($6.41 and $4.80) for a couple of months. A £2.99 wine is too cheap for some people, but a £4.99 one reduced to £2.99 is somehow acceptable. And surprise: at least as much wine is sold during those two promotion months as in the other ten months. The average price paid per bottle is then £3.99 or less, and both the producer and the retailer are making a decent profit on this.

This begs the question: was it *really* a £4.99 wine in the first place? Answer: no. Moreover, where such promotions were once rare occurrences, they now seem to dominate UK supermarket sales. And because only large wine companies have the volumes necessary to cater for these offers, the good little guys – whose £4.99 wines actually merit the £4.99 price tag – get elbowed off the shelves. Once again, the result is less choice, more blandness.

By all means, try the wines "on special". There's a glut of wine around the world at the moment, and the BOGOF (buy one, get one free) offers and pounds- or dollars-off deals will be with us for the foreseeable future. But don't think you're getting a bargain. You're simply paying the market rate.

5 | it doesn't look very new to me

just where and what is the new world?

More wine jargon, now. After all, wine is the language of love, of poetry, of... (That's enough gibberish – Ed.). So – tah dah! – step forward, the New World.

> The phrase "New World" originally encompassed just North and South America, but in wine geography, it also takes in Australia, New Zealand, and South Africa.

However, the term "New World" extends in its implications beyond geography. Allow me to elaborate.

> First, let's take a look at "Old World" wines: those from the traditional wine-producing regions of Europe – Bordeaux, the Mosel, Tuscany, Rioja, and so on.

Examine the label of a typical traditional bottle of Old World wine, and it will tell you first of all where it's from, then who has made it. The grape variety(ies) used? Probably not. A description and serving suggestions on the back label? You'll be lucky. But why should you need them? This, after all, is Monsieur Dupont's Puligny-Montrachet, or Signor Del

Ponte's Barbaresco; doesn't that tell you everything you need to know? Well, perhaps if you've been brought up on such wines, it does. But if you haven't…

Step forward New World wines. The New World countries have been making wine for decades; even New Zealand has been growing vines for not far short of 200 years. Yet they've really come into their own in the past thirty years. There are several reasons why.

1. Reliability. New World winemakers are technically adept, sticklers for hygiene, and make very few faulty wines.

2. Good Value. In order to establish a presence in other markets, the wines have been very sensibly priced.

3. Flavour. Many New World wine regions are warmer than their Old World counterparts, and thus grow riper, sweeter grapes. These then translate into more user-friendly flavours – people often say that you can "taste the sunshine".

4. Accessibility. Those who stumble over Old World terms like Trockenbeerenauslese and Montepulciano d'Abruzzo have no problem asking for a bottle of Montana Chardonnay.

5. Communication. New World producers talk to each other, share ideas, and realize that while they are competitors, it is in everybody's best interest to build Brand Chile, or Brand South Africa, or Brand California.

6. The Old World simply lost the plot. It rested on its laurels, churned out too many unreliable, poorly packaged wines, and didn't take the threat from the New World seriously until it found itself being displaced from the shop shelves.

> Today, the boundary between the New and Old Worlds is getting a little less precise.

Canny New World producers have realized that the place the grapes are grown (more of this in Chapter 9) can have a significant impact on a wine's quality. They've also realized that that there is such a thing as wines that are *too* hygienic – clean is good, sterile is not.

Meanwhile, many of their Old World counterparts have upgraded their cellars, adapted their vineyards so they can grow better, riper fruit, and have even taken a few lessons in marketing. New has become older, Old has become newer. Perhaps it's time to start talking about the Middle-Aged World (or is that something from Tolkien?).

all about wine part 2

back to basics

6 | well red

the ten greatest red grapes

Cabernet Sauvignon – *the head honcho.* This most
widely travelled of grapes manages to preserve its chewy
cassis, plum, and sometimes mint and cedar flavours
wherever it's planted. Hints of olives and blackberries crop
up in wines from warmer climates, while in cooler spots
you may find nuances of green peppers.

Pinot Noir – *moody but magnificent.* Great Pinot, no
longer the sole property of Burgundy, is seductive, fragrant,
absolutely delicious wine oozing flavours of red fruits,
undergrowth, and more. Grungy Pinot is boring and
overpriced. For every bottle of the former, expect at least
three of the latter.

Syrah/Shiraz – *the great pretender.* More reliable then
Pinot, more exciting than Cabernet, with Syrah ("Shiraz"
in the New World), you can have your cake and eat it,
too. Inky in colour with black pepper, blackberry, and
cassis flavours, plus occasional chocolate, orange peel,
and plum.

Merlot – *a friendly fellow.* Think of Merlot as a softer,
less formal Cabernet Sauvignon; indeed, the two are
often blended, with Merlot plumping out the more
angular Cabernet. Plums, blackberries, and cassis are
typical notes, while chocolate and blackberry leaf
are also common.

Grenache – *a taste of the warm south.* Light in colour, but rich in warm strawberry and herb flavours, Grenache is the driving force behind a whole host of wines in southern France and northern Spain, including Châteauneuf-du-Pape, Côtes-du-Rhône and Priorat. Increasingly popular elsewhere, and often blended with Syrah and Mourvèdre.

Tempranillo – *Rioja round the clock.* The main grape of Spain's Rioja and Ribera del Duero is slowly beating its spicy, strawberry-ish path to other countries. Expect to see more of this potential star in the future.

Nebbiolo – *there's no place like home.* Maybe it's car sickness, but Nebbiolo seldom strays beyond Piedmont, in northwest Italy. Yet there it makes splendid, long-lasting Barolo and Barbaresco – tar, roses, violets, raspberries, and wood-smoke are typical tasting notes.

Sangiovese – *by Jove!* Sangiovese has clocked up slightly more frequent-flyer points than Nebbiolo, but it's still a local boy at heart – in this instance in Tuscany, home of Chianti and Brunello di Montalcino. Think sour cherries, cassis, and fresh tobacco.

Cabernet Franc – *the other Cabernet.* A more leafy, tar-scented version of its relative Cabernet Sauvignon. Often used in blends with its more famous sibling, but capable of yielding refreshing, juicy, red wine by itself.

Malbec – *down Argentina way.* Its home is southwest France, but we have the Argentinians to thank for Malbec's current popularity. Capable of everything from friendly barbecue reds to powerful, age-worthy reds, all the while oozing mulberry and violet-scented fruit.

7 | all white on the night
the ten greatest white grapes

Chardonnay – *still crazy after all these years.* The ubiquitous Chardonnay can range from fabulous to foul, depending on the producer. Flavours, often tinged with and occasionally swamped by oak, vary from plump and tropical-fruity in warm climates to just-ripe melon and lemon in cool ones.

Riesling – *blue-blooded.* An aristocratic grape, at home both in the cool of Germany's Mosel Valley and in the warmer climes of South Australia. Dessert styles are unctuous yet balanced; dry ones are pithy and crisp, with apple and citrus-fruit flavours. Also shows terroir-character like no other variety (*see* page 30).

Sauvignon Blanc – *from fennel to feline.* A love-it-or-hate-it grape, the cocktail of gooseberries, asparagus, herbs, lemons, and cat pee (yes, really) can be overwhelming, but top examples from France's Loire Valley, New Zealand, and South Africa can be wonderfully refreshing.

Pinot Gris/Grigio – *fashion victim.* At its spicy best in Alsace, eastern France, making smoky, pineapple-and-peach wines. Also good in a lighter, nutty style in northeastern Italy, but too many versions here (and elsewhere in the world) fall under the heading of CFDN: crisp, fresh, dry, and neutral.

Sémillon – *please, don't let me be misunderstood.* Sémillon (without the é in Australia) can be rather neutral when young, but emerges phoenix-like with bottle-age to show a rich, toasty face with a lemony smile. Often used to add "grunt" to the more aromatic Sauvignon Blanc.

Gewürztraminer – *not a shy guy.* Providing the winemaker can rein in the ginger, lychee, rosewater, and orange flavours, Gewürz (without the ü in Alsace) is one of wine's most invigorating experiences. If he or she can't, however, then you're in cheap-perfume territory.

Viognier – *come up and see me some time.* Not as camp as Gewürztraminer, but just as aromatic, decent Viognier is heady and rich, and tastes like peaches, apricots, and hazelnuts. A pain to grow, though, as numerous under-flavoured examples demonstrate.

Muscat – *it tastes like what?* Yes, a rare grape that tastes like… well, *grapes.* It's often used for chocolate-friendly sweet wines, but is just as capable of making lightly spicy whites.

Chenin Blanc – *the agony and the ecstasy.* Used in France's Loire Valley for everything from buttock-clenchingly acidic, dry whites to some of the world's finest and longest-lived sweet wines. South African and Australian versions are gentler and richer. Apple, quince, nut, and honey are the good tasting notes; rotten eggs and vomit are less complimentary.

Palomino – *ma sherry amour.* Not heard of Palomino? The name doesn't feature on many bottles, but it is the main grape in that most underrated of all wines, sherry.

8 | a vine romance

exactly what does go on in the vineyard?

Wine 101. Wine is made from grapes, and grapes grow
in vineyards. Pretty obvious, really. So you just plant
a grape seed and then wait for the little fellows to appear,
right? Nope. It's more a case of Why? Where? What?
How? When?

Why? It's nearly impossible to have both quality and
quantity, so what is the producer trying to make – great wine
by the thimbleful, grotty wine by the bucketful or something
in-between? Once that's decided, then it's a case of…

Where? Great wine can only come from great vineyards
(more of that later), and these are few and far between.
They're not cheap, either; parts of Burgundy are more
expensive than Manhattan. At the high-volume end of the
scale, large tracts of reasonably uniform, tractor-friendly
land are needed. In both instances, there needs to be
enough water, either falling as rain, or pumped through
irrigation systems.

What? Cabernet Sauvignon? Chardonnay? Syrah? Maybe
all three and more besides? Growers plant cuttings rather
than seeds (it's just more reliable) and they can get these
either from the local Vines 'R' Us plant nursery or by

propagating cuttings from other vineyards. Because of a lousy louse called phylloxera that loves eating vine roots, the cuttings in most parts of the world come grafted onto rootstocks. Above the ground, the plant may be Merlot; below, it's a completely different type of vine that is phylloxera-resistant.

How? How far apart should the vines be? Too close together, and the foliage shades the grapes on a neighbouring plant. Too far apart, and space is wasted. How should they be trained? A vine needs enough leaves for photosynthesis, but not so many that the grapes can't see the sun. How hard should they be pruned? Well, do you want small amounts of highly flavoured grapes, or lots of more dilute ones? How much mechanization will there be? Many jobs, including harvesting, can be done by machine, but the vineyard has to be planted accordingly. How much, if any, fertilizer, herbicide, and fungicide should be used? That's enough of the "Hows" for the moment. Finally…

When? Some people fit their vineyard work in around other activities; others plan it according to the phases of the moon, and still others do it with an intuition born of generations of experience. Harvesting is the most critical of jobs. There are several scientific ways of determining the time for picking, but the best way is simply to go out in the vineyards and taste the grapes. If they taste ripe, then it's time to pick.

9 | talking dirty
what is terroir?

No, not terrier, not terror; the term terroir (pronounced *tearrrr-wahhh*) encompasses all the natural elements that can affect a vine, such as the composition of the soil, the climate, the altitude, aspect, and slope of the vineyard, and the surrounding geography. For confirmed Old Worlders (*see* Chapter 5), terroir is everything in a wine. For staunch New Worlders, it is a lame excuse to charge way too much for faulty wine. The truth lies somewhere between these two extremes.

How does terroir show itself in a wine? Take away the flavours of the grape variety, take away the flavours that can be attributed to the winemaker (more of that later), and what remains is a result of the terroir.

> Geographic and climatic influences are undeniable. Wines from higher altitudes tend to be crisper than those from lower ones. Wines from vineyards on slopes angled towards the midday sun will be riper than those facing away.

The impact of the soil is more controversial, but for Old Worlders, it is perhaps the most important aspect of terroir.

There might be an **earthy note,** maybe a **hint** of **stone – flint, slate, or volcanic lava,** for example.

And sometimes a nuance that you can't pin down: "minerality" is the word on such occasions.

> `There's no science that shows`
> `how elements in the soil can end`
> `up in a wine.`

However, my glass of Riesling from the slate slopes overlooking the river Mosel in Germany has more than a little slatey tang.

And what if you can't taste the soil? Maybe the terroir didn't have much character anyway. Nothing wrong with that, providing the price is right. Or, more worrying, the producer didn't manage to transfer its character to the bottle; this could be the result of sloppy winemaking.

Too much oak is the **big culprit here** (if you want an overdose of wood, chew a pencil – just keep it out of my wine).

Or it could be **high yields.** The more **grapes** a **vine is asked to produce,** the **less** will be their **flavour.**

Or it could be a **bad diet.** If a vine gets its **nourishment** from **fertilizers,** and its **water** from an **irrigation pipe**, then the **soil** is almost **irrelevant.**

To experience the highs and lows
of terroir, head for Burgundy,
where there are hundreds of
vineyards, each (allegedly) with
its own unique character.

In the good cellars, the nuances of the different terroirs
shine through in the various wines. In the bad ones, you
wonder why someone has the nerve to charge megabucks for
overoaked, underflavoured wines that are hard to tell apart.

10 | first, catch your grapes
exactly what goes on in the winery?

Grapes go in at one end of the winery; bottles of wine
come out at the other. Let's see what happens in between
– red wines first.

Crushing/De-stemming. Grape stalks (ever bitten into one?)
can contain harsh tannins and bitter oils, so the grapes are
usually tipped into a machine that removes the stems and
then does a light crushing to split the skins.

Fermenting. Fermenting vessels may be anything from small
wooden barrels with open tops to honking great stainless-steel
tanks with lids. Non-chemists: take a nap for the next few lines.

> In fermentation, yeasts act on sugar
> to produce alcohol and CO_2.

The sugar ideally comes from grape juice, although in cooler
climes it might have to be added to boost the alcohol. The
yeast usually comes from a packet, although some winemakers
prefer to let yeasts naturally present in the air and on the
grapeskins do the business; it's risky, but can result in wines
with more character. Fermentation produces lots of heat, so
the vat or tank may have a built-in refrigeration system. The
ferment needs to be warm enough to extract all the flavours,

but not so high that the yeasts can't work. The cooler the ferment, the slower it proceeds. Also, CO_2 pushes the grape-skins to the top, so there has to be a way of making sure this "cap" is mixed back in with the juice regularly. This can be done by pumping juice up and over from the bottom of the tank. Occasionally, someone strips off and treads the mush.

Macerating. Once fermentation is over, the new wine is often left in contact with the grapeskins for anything up to three weeks in order to extract even more flavour. It's a bit like making tea: the longer it steeps, the stronger the tea.

Pressing. The free-run juice, as it's called, is then drained off, leaving the grapeskins. These are transferred to a press and squeezed to make the press wine. Sometimes this is blended with free-run juice, sometimes not.

Maturation. Deserves its own chapter – *see* next section.

White wine is different. The aim is to get the juice off the grapeskins as quickly as possible, as too much "skin contact" can impart a bitter flavour (although a small amount adds character). So the process is:

Destem, then crush, do any skin contact, drain the juice off and perhaps allow it to settle, then transfer it to a vat for fermentation (much cooler than for red wine). After that, it's on to maturation…

11 | oaky-dokey

or how raw, adolescent wines turn into more mature, interesting adults

We now have a brand-new wine. What's stopping us from bottling it and shipping it out to sell? That's what happens to many wines. They may sit for a while in a tank, to let all the sludgy bits settle to the bottom. To speed this process up, they may be "fined" – no, not for speeding or dropping litter. Fining involves adding a fining agent to make a wine less hazy.

Filtration can also be used to remove other unwanted particles. However, overzealous fining and filtration can also strip out part of the flavour, and some producers prefer to let the wine clear naturally – look for the words "Unfined" and/or "Unfiltered" on bottles.

And for the wines that aren't to be bottled right away? Some stay in a tank, maybe with some of the sludgy bits (the "lees") so they can pick up more flavour. The tanks need to be kept fairly chilly, or the wine will age too quickly.

> Which brings me to an aside. If you ever wondered why many Mediterranean regions have only recently got their wine-acts together, it's because very few wineries had any cool storage.

But many wines go into oak barrels for their maturation. A barrel has two main effects on wine.

Firstly, *flavour.* The newer and smaller the barrel, the more it will influence the wine.

> Coconut, vanilla, cloves, and toast are
> the most common **wood-related flavours.**

If money is tight, you can simply buy massive, tea-bag-like affairs full of oak chips, or "curtains" of oak staves (called "tank planks") which can be plonked into the fermenting and ageing tanks to add an oaky flavour.

The second effect is more subtle. A barrel isn't 100 per cent airtight, and the wine "breathes" through the pores in the oak. The fruit flavours become less boisterous, the colour becomes more stable, and the wine becomes more mellow and (hopefully) more interesting. Just how long a wine spends in wood varies from wine to wine – and from winemaker to winemaker. Some white wines, Chardonnays especially, are even fermented in oak.

Just a final word on malolactic fermentation (MLF or "malo" for short), which involves the conversion of malic acid (think apples) to lactic acid (think milk). In layman's terms, it makes for softer wines. Most red wines go through malo, normally towards the end of or just after alcoholic fermentation. With whites, malo can add a buttery richness, and is popular with many winemakers. Others, however, prefer to suppress it, especially in warm regions where the wine is soft enough already. Also, certain varieties such as Riesling don't take kindly to malo (or to oak, for that matter).

12 | a question of style

the low-down on sparkling, fortified, and other wine styles

Sparkling wines. Is making sparkling wines simply a matter of pumping your burgundy full of bubbles? Some cheaper bubblies are made in precisely this way. However, most are made by adding a mixture of yeast and sugar to a ready-made still wine to initiate a new fermentation. If the released CO_2 is prevented from escaping, it will dissolve in the wine, making it fizzy. Sometimes (in Champagne, for example), this second fermentation takes place in the bottle, but large tanks can also be used. The wine sits on its yeasty sludge – those lees again – acquiring extra flavours in the process. The lees are then removed (this isn't essential, but who wants cloudy fizz?), and the wine is ready to be bottled (if it wasn't in bottle already) and corked. Prior to corking, a *dosage*, or syrupy mixture of older wine and sugar, is often added to smooth out any rough edges. Oh, and by the way:

Sparklers don't have to be white.

Rosé bubbly, made either by blending a dollop of red wine in with a white, or by only draining the juice off the skins of the red grapes before it has picked up too much colour, is *de rigeur* for some weddings. And in Australia, no self-respecting Christmas dinner is complete without a bottle or six of sparkling red, usually made from Shiraz.

Fortified wines. Alcohol has been added to these wines. This stops the yeast working, so the earlier you add the spirit, the sweeter the wine will be (= more unfermented sugar). Sometimes the spirit is added just as fermentation starts – Pineau des Charentes is the best-known example.

Port is fortified halfway through its fermentation and splits roughly into two camps: those bottled early to retain fruit (ruby, vintage), and those bottled after a lengthy spell in a barrel (tawny), when the fruit is more raisin-like and the colour has veered from purple to red-brown. Sherries are fortified at the end of fermentation, when the wine is dry.

> Sherry is weird. As with fizz, the base wines aren't especially tasty; it's the sherry-fication that does the magic.

Fino and manzanilla sherries get their pungent, bready flavour from ageing in cask under a blanket of a white mould called *flor*. When the *flor* gives up, the wine becomes an amontillado. If the *flor* doesn't develop, the wine can still age in cask, but it will become not a fino but a nutty oloroso. Got all that? No; it still confuses me at times. Just remember that all sherries are dry to begin with, but sometimes they'll be blended with sweeter wines or grape juice to create sweeter styles.

Non-alcoholic wine. The operative word here is "avoid". If you want a drink without alcohol, fruit juice is cheaper and tastier. Even water is better.

13 | organic wine

lean, mean, and green

Forget beards, beads, and Birkenstocks; the modern organic wine producer looks no different from his non-organic counterpart. The difference lies in their respect for the environment. Our Jolly Green Giant eschews the artificial fertilizers, herbicides, and fungicides that others just pile on their vineyards, and prefers to let nature have its way, aided from time to time with a dash of sheep shit (and cow, and chicken).

In parts of the world where the sun shines and there isn't much rain, this is relatively easy. In cooler, soggier climes where humidity and rainfall often give rise to fungal diseases, it's much more of a challenge, although not an impossibility – even England can muster a handful of organic wines.

> For a wine to be labelled as organic, it has to meet the standards set by one of a number of monitoring bodies around the world.

These control not only what happens in the vineyard but what goes on in the winery as well. Some additives are allowed, others are not. Sulphur, the winemaker's disinfectant, is permitted, but only in small doses.

Is organic wine better than non-organic? Better for the environment, certainly, and better for our health, yes (who wants a wine with pesticide residue in it?). But is it necessarily better wine? No.

> There are **good** and **bad organic wines**, and their **quality** comes down to the **producer** rather than to their **organic-ness**.

One step beyond organic is biodynamic. Biodynamic farming conducts the various vineyard operations according to the phases of the moon. If that's not weird enough, how about fermenting dandelion heads in a cow's stomach, and then mixing them with manure and water in a "vortex"? Or burying a cow's horn full of manure for the winter and then spraying the contents in minute amounts over the vineyard? It sounds like the most mumbo of jumbos, but – well, it seems to work, although no one knows precisely why. Several of the world's finest producers have now switched to full-time biodynamic farming, and many others are following suit.

And what about vegetarian and vegan wines? Isn't wine made from *grapes*? Yes, of course it is. However, there are some non-grape products involved in wine production. Remember fining agents from Chapter 11? Some are derived from clay, but several others in use are of animal origin, among them gelatine, egg whites, casein (a milk protein), and isinglass, which comes from, of all things, fish bladders (how on earth did they discover that this worked?).

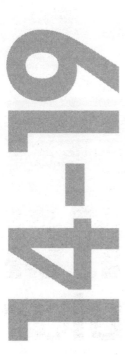

where to go to find out more

extra
curricular

14 | merchant of vinous

how to track down a decent wine shop

Ten ways of spotting the good from the bad and the ugly.

1. Does the range change regularly? Time was when traditional wine merchants would change their ranges maybe once or twice a year. The best outfits now often buy in parcels so small that they're in and out of stock within a month, sometimes a week. And if you ask them why they don't produce a wine list, they'll say, "What's the point? It would be out of date as soon as it had been printed."

2. Do the wines come from lots of different producers? If the wines from, say, Burgundy, the Rhône and southern France all carry the name of the same producer, then some folk are being lazy in their buying habits.

3. Are the wines the same ones you've seen in the supermarkets? Nothing wrong with supermarket wines, or indeed, with the odd famous brand or two. But if the same old wines monopolize the shelves, then again: someone isn't being as thorough as he or she could be. However...

4. Get the feeling you're being had? In other words, is that unfamiliar label just an excuse for the merchant to bump up the price of a so-so wine? Tasting is the only way to find out.

5. Are they afraid to specialize? Why should someone with a passion for Greek wine stock Rioja? Would you rather buy from someone single-minded or a jack-of-all-trades?

6. Does anything in the range look like it should be put out to pasture? Better shops should have a reasonably quick stock turnover. Anything not moving as swiftly as it should may well end up in the January sales.

7. When you ask staff members a question, does wine seep out of their pores? Or do they simply pick up the bottle and read out what it says on the back?

8. Do they always try to steer you towards more expensive wines? A decent wine merchant will be as proud of his selection of lower-priced wines as of anything at his higher prices. Of course, he wants you to spend as much money as possible, but the good guys will be much more interested in building a long-term relationship with you than in getting you to cough up just once in a big way.

9. If there's a shop, does it feel like the sort of place where a bottle would be happy for several weeks? Or does the temperature inside yo-yo up and down while the wine cooks slowly under harsh fluorescent lights?

10. Do they hold regular tastings for customers? Are they confident enough in their selections to be able to let you try before you buy? If not, why not?

15 | press wine

how to spot a wine writer with your best interests at heart

A decent wine column should educate and entertain in equal measures.

> It should make you want to grab a glass and take a slurp, rush out and buy a dozen bottles or so, jet off to that secluded vineyard surrounded by olive groves and bathed in sun from dawn to dusk.

But how many conform to such a description? Not enough. What we have instead are columns that amount to not much more than shopping lists for cheap, widely available wine. Sometimes, it's not the writers who are to blame.

> Often, they are merely puppets for editors who take a short-sighted view of wine, and shun everything that smacks of the vaguely esoteric.

Imagine if the same approach were applied to the automotive section ("You can't do Porsches, Ferraris, or Aston Martins; give me 1,200 words on which garage

has the cheapest fuel."). Or the food pages ("Never mind Umbrian single-estate organic olive oils; who sells the best baked beans?").

Now, people *are*, of course, interested in everyday matters such as baked beans and fuel prices and cut-price Merlot. But that's not *all* they're interested in.

> A good wine column should be gently evangelistic in its tone, looking at the familiar, but also finding time to move people out of the comfort zone into unexplored territory.

The wine geeks are going to read it regardless of the subject matter, but the balancing act – achieved by few – is to appeal to those with a more casual interest.

Five ways to spot a bad wine column.

1. The same old producers and retailers crop up time after time. How impartial is the advice?

2. You need a PhD in wine to understand it. An occasional unfamiliar term is fine, providing it is explained in layman's terms. A column full of them is a turn-off.

3. It is afraid to recommend expensive wine. We might drive a Ford, but we don't mind reading about Lamborghinis every once in a while.

4. It contains outlandish statements. An inexpensive Viognier may very well embarrass wines at two or three times the price. Asking readers to believe that it is the best Viognier in the world is a bridge too far.

5. It recommends wines you don't like. Wine writers are critics, and critics disagree from time to time. But if none of the recommendations hits the right buttons for you, then find a new critic.

16 | don't medal with me
the ins and outs of wine competitions

Watch out: here comes Medallion Vin, a wine so weighed down with medals that it has trouble walking. Surely something so bedecked with gold, silver, and bronze must be a wine among wines, a true thoroughbred. Well, maybe. Then again, maybe not...

The idea of wine competitions is a good one. Bottles jostle with each other to see who comes out on top. The winners go on to glory while the losers mutter and curse, and wonder how they could do better next time. The marketing folk love wine shows. Sales of Domaine Blob Cabernet Sauvignon will soar if it gets a top medal, and all it costs is the entry fee – not cheap, but certainly cheaper than a major ad campaign – and a few bottles of wine.

And since those sampling the wines have no idea whose wines they're tasting (*see* Chapter 26), today's shows provide a completely fair fight. A wine from a tiny vineyard where production is measured in hundreds of cases has just as much chance of winning a top award as another from a global conglomerate for whom the words "limited edition" mean that the wine is only available in twelve countries.

But (and you knew there was a "but" coming) wine, like art and literature, isn't a finish-line subject, so there's no scientific definition of what constitutes the best in the world. Put the same set of wines in front of two different panels of tasters, or even the same panel of tasters on a different day, and then take a look at the results. Are they similar? Probably. But the same? Probably not.

The wines that tend to perform well in competitions are the "loud" ones.

In a line-up of **sixty Chardonnays** – not uncommon in many shows – the ones that are the **sweetest, ripest** and/or **oakiest** often **rise to the top**, while the **more subtle wines get lost.**

Then there's the problem of quirky wines, ones that are brilliant in their style but controversial. It only takes one panel member to pan them, and they end up with a bronze medal rather than a gold. The upshot is that the producers of quirky or subtle wines are less inclined to enter competitions. So, too, are those who make highly acclaimed wines that sell out each year, regardless of success in the shows. In the Olympics, all the top names compete. In wine shows, they don't.

On the whole, though, wine competitions are a "good thing": encouraging new talent and promoting the whole topic of wine. Faced with two similar-looking but unknown bottles, opting for the one with the medal is a smart move.

But when you see something dubbed "The Best Red Wine in the World", take it with a pinch of salt.

17 | oenologue-ing on
the tangled world wide web of wine

Plug the word "wine" into your favourite internet search engine, and it will find literally millions of sites. Take out those which begin with riveting phrases such as, "Wine is an Open Source implementation of the Windows API on top of X and Unix" and there are still loads that relate to all matters grapey.

Not sure where to start? Well, here are a dozen or so of my favourites.

Let's talk. Talking about wine online isn't the same as drinking the stuff, but for many people it's a pleasant interlude. There are several forums and newsgroups. Three stand out.

The Wine Lovers Discussion Group on Robins Garr's *www.wineloverspage.com*

Marks Squires' Wine Bulletin Board on *www.erobertparker.com* (itself worth exploring) attracts a mainly American audience.

Brits may prefer the very active **UK Wine Forum** on Tom Cannavan's excellent *www.wine-pages.com*

Hot off the press! For all the latest wine-related news stories, two sites, both with extensive archives, take some beating:

www.winebusiness.com/news
www.vintners.com
(click on the "Industry news" button.)

Slightly cooler off the press, but still nice and warm.
Of the terrestrial wine magazines with their own sites, the two best are:

www.decanter.com
www.winespectator.com
Both are packed with information, news, reviews and more.

A full-access subscription to *The Wine Spectator* site costs US$49.95 per year, but the basic package will be fine for most folk.

Where can I find...? If you're trying to track down a particular wine, or wondering where you can buy wines from your dad's birth year, then:

www.wine-searcher.com

is the place to look. You have to pay for the Pro version (US$24.95 a year in summer 2003), but the regular (free) version is adequate for most queries.

Let me entertain you. Thousands of wineries now have websites. Few have entertaining ones. Two of the most inspiring are the brainchildren of off-the-wall Californians.

On *www.wine-maker.net*, Sean Thackrey goes well beyond the here-are-my-wines formula and offers transcriptions of many historic winemaking texts dating back to the ancient Greeks and Romans.

Meanwhile *www.bonnydoonvineyard.com* is as wacky, weird, and wonderful as its creator Randall Grahm (and his wines).

Also worth the surf is supremely entertaining Silly Tasting Notes Generator at:

www.gmon.com/tech/output.shtml

Just click the button, and out they come: "Premature but understated Syrah. Strong, pungent spore, corpulent yellow taffy, and lingering pesto. Drink now through 2006."

And finally... If you still need an online wine fix, then check out Dean Tudor's mammoth and regularly updated list of links at:

www.ryerson.ca/~dtudor/www.htm

If it's not here, it's probably not worth the click.

18 | society occasions

the pros and cons of the local wine society

Tasting and talking about wines with other people is an excellent way to expand the horizons of "what I like", and there are now many classes and courses on the subject. These may be run in conjunction with a local wine merchant, they may be part of an adult education programme, or they may just be some chums getting together for a weekly session.

Where once the typical member of a wine class would have been a fifty-five-year-old man in a shabby brown sweater, most groups are now much more cosmopolitan. There are more women. There are more people under twenty-five. There might even be some women under twenty-five. It shouldn't take much legwork to find out what's on offer in your neck of the woods (in the way of classes, not women under twenty-five…).

The success of the group depends on the wines you're tasting and who's in charge. If it's run by a wine merchant or a local college, chances are that you won't have any control over either; if it's not for you, vote with your feet.

If you are able to run your own tastings, that's a different matter. Here are a couple of tips.

Keep a list of what you've tasted, as this will show what you've done to death, and what you've missed out on. Did we really need to try Australian wines every third week? Why do all the Riojas we taste come from the same shop? How come we've never done a tasting of port/sherry/Austrian wines? And when are we going to try some really expensive wines? When you plan your next round of tastings, you can then try to fill in the gaps. Many merchants are willing to put together tasting cases, often at a discount. They'll also supply information on the wines and may even send someone along to help run it.

The best wine groups talk a lot. Encourage the shy ones and dampen down those who are not short of opinions.

19 | grape-grazing
visiting wineries

If you're lucky, you may have wineries near where you live. If not, at some point you may travel in a wine region. Whichever, here are the ten ins and outs of visiting a winery.

1. Business as usual. Some wineries can cater to loads of tourists; others can't. Find out beforehand whether visitors are actively welcomed or merely tolerated. If you're going to turn up at a small winery unannounced, don't expect the proprietor to give you two hours of his undivided attention.

2. There's no such thing as a free lunch. Pouring wine down people's throats may be good PR, but it's expensive, and there's now a fee for tasting at some wineries. If there isn't, and you leave empty-handed having slurped your way through half a dozen wines, don't be surprised if your farewell isn't received with great enthusiasm. However…

3. Don't leave your critical faculties in the car. They might be trying to get you to open your wallet, but crap wine is crap wine, and it'll taste worse when you get it home. If you genuinely don't like anything, don't feel obliged to buy.

4. Breakfast of champions. If they ask for feedback, be honest. Why tell them you love their oaky Chardonnay when it really makes you gag? It'll only encourage them to make more.

5. Move along, please. There's nothing as annoying at a winery as people who sprawl across the counter and don't let anyone else near the wines. Get your sample of wine and move away, or risk a kick in the pants.

6. Limited appeal. Look for limited-edition wines, or older wines that have sold out in the stores. Often the cellar door is the only place you'll find such things.

7. Paying through the nosé for the rosé. You'd think that the wines would be cheaper to buy from the winery than in the shops. And they probably are at the farm gate in Europe. But at the gleaming new visitors centre in California or Australia, they might even be more expensive.

8. The long and winding road. Even if you're spitting all the wines out – and let's face it: few people do – some ends up going down your throat. If you don't want to end up in a ditch, make sure you have someone sober to drive you around.

9. Transports of delight. You bought three bottles at the first winery, four at the second, a case at the third... All well and good if you'll be driving home, but if you're not, where are you going to put them on the plane?

10. Er, can't think of a tenth. Time for the next chapter.

every
what you need besides bottles of wine
home
should
have one

20 | glass act
tracking down decent wineglasses

Let's go to glass extremes. The Austrian company Riedel produces dozens of different, beautiful, and rather expensive (not to mention fragile) styles of glasses, each of which is deemed ideal for a particular type of wine. A marketing gimmick?

> The wines do actually **taste different** in the **various glasses**, and in the **"right" glass**, they taste **significantly better** than in the **"wrong" one.**

In an ideal world, maybe we'd all have the money and storage space to have a wide selection of "stemware" (dreadful term). But we don't.

Cut to the newly equipped kitchen, complete with state-of-the-art oven, a fridge that could hold a moose, and an espresso machine to die for. Someone has obviously forked out some serious cash here, yet open one of the cupboards and what do you find? Eight chipped wine glasses that were given away to loyal customers by the local supermarket five years ago.

This is simply a crime, especially when the kitchen's owners don't object to splurging on expensive hooch every now and then.

You don't have to spend Riedel-money in order to get a decent wineglass. Here's what to look for in an ideal, everyday vessel.

1. A decent measure of wine should come less than halfway up the glass. We'll see why in Chapter 26.

2. It should taper toward the rim. Think of a capital "U" with the top edges squeezed together slightly. Think of a horseshoe. Think of a magnet.

3. It should have a long enough stem for you to be able to hold it without touching the bowl of the glass. Hands warm up wine and leave fingerprints.

4. It shouldn't have any patterns. Apologies to those who have inherited great-granny's set of cut-glass vessels; save them for elderflower cordial.

5. It should be dishwasher-proof. No real wine reason for this; I'm just lazy.

Special glasses for port and sherry? No. They're wines, so treat them as such. You might want some taller glasses ("flutes" in winespeak) for sparkling wines – the bubbles look nice in them – but even these are fine in normal glasses.

As for special occasions, by all means invest in swankier glasses; the Riedel Chianti Classico glass is a good all-rounder. But whatever you choose, the above rules (apart from 5.) apply.

21 | tools of the trade

all about corkscrews, foil-cutters, wine coolers, and more

Bottle. Glass. Corkscrew. Do wine-lovers need anything else to get to grips with the beverage of their choice? "Need", maybe not, but there are several gadgets out there that people seem to want push in our direction. How useful are they?

Corkscrews first. Even with the growth of screwcaps (*see* page 69), every home should have one. No – two, at least (they have a habit of disappearing). Which you choose depends on how many bottles you're planning to open, and what your budget is.

> If money is no object, the Lever-
> Action Screwpull, that comes
> in Regular and chrome-laden
> Professional versions, is the Big
> Daddy of corkscrews.

Handsome, efficient (just like me – *not*) but not cheap. There are now several look-alikes at a fraction of the price. Some of them work well, others don't. If possible, ask for a road test before you buy one.

For pocket-sized corkscrews, the cheaper models from Screwpull work well. So, too, do the waiter's friends, which use a lever mechanism to get purchase on the cork. The recently introduced "Pulltaps" version, where

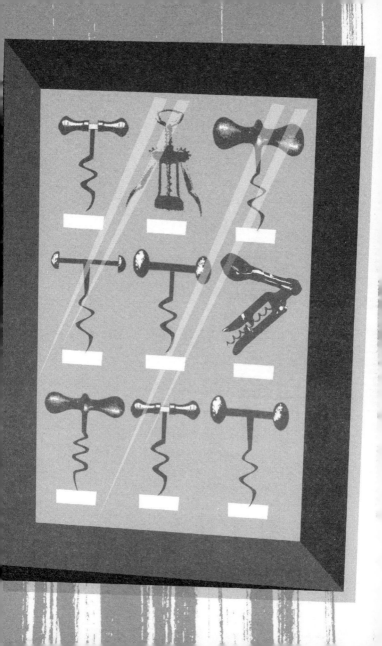

there are two fulcrums (fulcra?) for the lever section, are especially good.

If you want one of the old robot-with-hairy-armpits corkscrews, make sure that the "worm" of the screw has a decent spiral. Those with a solid core can just pull the centre out of the corks.

Then there are gadgets that fall into the "not essential but desirable" bracket.

You can use a knife to remove the capsule from bottles, but a purpose-built foil-cutter does the job much better. Buy a Screwpull and one might even come with it in the box.

Cooling sleeves (those from Vacuvin are the most common) are useful for rapidly chilling wine.

Keep them in **the freezer** until they're needed, then **simply slip them over the bottle** and wait a **few minutes.**

It's far better than sticking the bottle in the freezer. Vacuvin also makes a device for preserving leftover wine. Insert one of the special stoppers, pump the special pump a few times, and the wine is protected by a vacuum – or that's the theory. Some swear by it, others are more sceptical. If I have a half-empty bottle of wine, I simply cork it up and put it in the fridge – even if it's red. In my experience, this works just as well as Vacuvin.

And as for other wine paraphernalia, like thermometers, drip stops, port tongs, and decanting cradles? You don't need them. Spend your money on wine instead.

22 | what a corker!
or, a tale of three sealing methods

Come with me, if you will, to a land where corks don't exist, and bottles of wines are stoppered by other methods.

One day, a seer appears, shouting, "Eureka! I have seen the future of wine closures, and it is called cork!"

"Tell us more about this wondrous new substance, o great one!" shout the citizens.

"Gladly I will," says Quercus Dumbledore, for that is his name. "You plant a tree, then after twenty-five years, strip all the bark from it, leave it stacked up for six months, boil it for an hour and a half, leave it for a further three weeks, then punch cylindrical pieces out of it and behold! Cork."

"Sounds like a bit of a slog, your Excellency," comes the reply. "But presumably you can cut the bark every year?"

"Not exactly," sighs Dumbledore. "You have to wait nine more years for the bark to grow back before you can do another harvest."

"Sounds like a lot of a slog," shouts the crowd. "So what's it got going for it?"

"Well," replies the maestro, "you may find that around one bottle in twenty has a rather musty smell associated with it, and that the other bottles don't all develop at the same pace. But the best part about it is… it makes a wonderful 'pop' when you pull it out of the bottle!"

And the people cried as one: "Get thee back to Hogwarts!"

Quercus Dumbledore may not exist, but problems with corks certainly do. If you've ever had a wine that smelled like the inside of a damp cupboard, then chances are it was "corked" – affected by a mould that has grown on the cork during its manufacture.

In many instances, the wine is so tainted as to be undrinkable. In others, the corkiness merely flattens out the aromas and flavours. Dissatisfaction with the consistency of corks (what other food-related product has a failure rate of two to ten per cent?) has understandably led several producers to look at alternatives.

Synthetic corks were the first to be in widespread use, but they're not perfect. They're tough to get out of the bottle (and in again, if you have some wine left), they're not biodegradable, and they've yet to prove how effective they are for long-term storage.

Screwcaps are a different matter. They're cheap, easy to dispose of, and have already shown that they can preserve a wine for twenty years and more. Many producers in Australia and New Zealand have switched to screwcaps, and several in other parts of the world are following suit.

You may not get the "pop!" of cork, but then, you don't get a faulty wine.

23 | off the shelf
the ten best wine books

Building your wine library? Here are some of my favourite books.

THREE HEAVYWEIGHTS

Oxford Companion to Wine, edited by Jancis Robinson (Oxford University Press, 2nd edition, 1999). Weighty in size and content, and unparalleled in its scope as a reference book, covering grape varieties, wine regions, the history of wine, viticulture, winemaking, and more.

The New Sotheby's Wine Encyclopaedia, Tom Stevenson (Dorling Kindersley, 4th edition, 2001). Another fine, comprehensive tome. This doesn't quite cover the same amount of ground as the *Oxford Companion*, but with more maps, illustrations, and producer recommendations, many will find this an easier read.

The World Atlas of Wine, Hugh Johnson & Jancis Robinson (Mitchell Beazley, 5th edition, 2001). A classic since it first appeared in 1971. The latest edition is as authoritative and erudite as ever, with completely new maps throughout.

THREE MIDDLEWEIGHTS

The New France, Andrew Jefford (Mitchell Beazley, 2002). A passionate book by a passionate man. Jefford's love for France, French wines, and terroir oozes from every page, and his writing is second to none in the wine world. Superb pics by Jason Lowe, too.

Grapes & Wines, Oz Clarke & Margaret Rand
(Little, Brown, 2001). Friendly guide through all the
major grape varieties, and dozens of less familiar ones, too.
Also excellent section on modern viticulture.
Burgundy, Anthony Hanson (Mitchell Beazley, 2003).
No better critique of any wine region exists than this
thorough, entertaining, opinionated, and well-written tome –
can we have another edition soon, please Mr H?

BEDTIME READING

Zin: the History and Mystery of Zinfandel, David
Darlington (Da Capo Press, 2001). Entertaining and
well-written story of California's own grape variety. You don't
have to be a Zin fan (del) to enjoy this. Originally published
under the much better title of *Angels' Visits*.
The Vintner's Luck, Elizabeth Knox (Victoria University
Press, 1998). A rare fine novel based around wine.
A magical and unpredictable love story set in
nineteenth century Burgundy with a twist in the tail.

ANCIENT AND MODERN

Vintage Wine, Michael Broadbent (Little, Brown, 2002).
No one has tasted more fine old wines than the still-sprightly
Broadbent. This is basically a book of tasting notes for wines
most of us will never ever come across, but it makes
fascinating reading nonetheless.
Parker's Wine Buyer's Guide, Robert M. Parker, Jr. (Dorling
Kindersley, 6th edition, 2002). Massive collection of profiles
and tasting notes from the world's most influential wine writer.

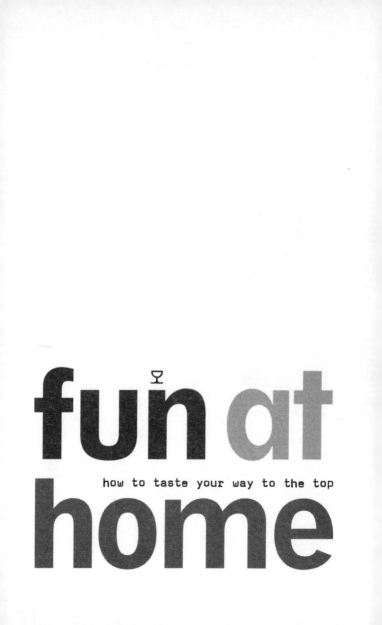

fun at home
how to taste your way to the top
home

24 | a taste of things to come
why not organize your own tasting?

Wine, of course, is meant to be drunk. So let's start on January 1 at the back of the wine shop and drink our way toward the checkout at the rate of three different bottles a week. Come December, you'll have sampled an impressive 156 wines – impressive, that is, until you realize that you've covered only about a quarter of the range. And since new wines appear while old ones disappear throughout the year, you're never going to be up to speed on what are the best wines on the shelf. Unless…

Unless you have the liver of an elephant? Probably not. Some people do manage a couple of bottles a day, but they're not usually doing it to experience the finer points of the wines. Unless you keep in touch with wine writers' recommendations? A better approach. Over the course of a year, the major retailers bombard wine hacks with lists, details of promotions, and invitations to tastings. But even we can't keep in touch with what all the stores are doing all the time.

But what about organizing your own tasting? Does that sound a bit pretentious? Only as pretentious as having your own gym equipment at home. The more you work out on your tasting at home, the less likely you are to have sand (of the metaphorical kind) kicked in your face in the wine shop.

So what do you need to get you started? Not much.

Some **wine...**

a **corkscrew...**

glass(es) (one for each wine if you can manage that, but not essential)**...**

somewhere to spit the wine out, if you think you might need it (buckets or kitchen sinks are fine)**...**

and possibly a **pen and paper** for any words of wisdom you feel prompted to write.

That's all you strictly need, but there's one other element that will make the whole shebang more informative and entertaining: company. Get some friends to join in, and not only will you have more fun, but you might even be able to get them to chip in for the wine.

```
Wine loosens the tongue, and while you
   all might shy away from talking about
   the various bottles initially, chances
   are that by the time the pizzas arrive,
             there'll be plenty of banter.
```

How seriously you take it is entirely up to you. You may want to see who can produce the most outlandish description; you may just want to see which was everyone's favourite. But if you get hooked on tasting, then the next few chapters are for you.

25 | compare & contrast

mini-tastings to show that all wines don't taste the same

Let's get back to that line of my mother's:

> "They all taste the same to me."

The most convincing way of showing her that they don't is to make her do what in winespeak is called a comparative tasting. It's a bit of a grand title, but all it means is trying a range of wines side by side and seeing what their differences are. Wine pros at wine shows can sometimes find themselves confronted with a hundred-strong line-up. However, such an array won't fit on the average kitchen table, so you're better off starting small – three wines is fine to begin with.

As for what to try, there are no hard and fast rules, but you'll learn more if there's a theme running through the wines.

The most common themed tastings even have their own names: vertical and horizontal.

In a vertical tasting, the idea is to look at the same wine, but from different years. This is quite a tough one to arrange, as most shops only stock the current vintage of each wine, but if you do find one with a few older bottles (and it looks like they've been stored well – *see* Chapter 14), it's certainly worth trying.

And horizontal? No, it's not a reference to the state you're in after a long vertical tasting. This is where you have similar wines from (ideally) the same vintage. If you're stuck for ideas for horizontal tastings, here are a few suggestions.

Price-based – *does paying more bucks get you louder bangs?*
Wines from the same region and grape variety(ies) but at different prices – low, medium, and high, for example.
If they come from the same producer, all the better.
Begin with: Australian Chardonnay.

Grape-based – *is variety the spice of life?* Similarly priced wines made from different grape varieties. Again, try to find the same producer and/or region, but this may be impossible; Pinotages outside South Africa, and Zinfandel outside California are thin on the ground. Begin with: Cabernet, Merlot, and Zinfandel from California.

Geographical – *tasting all over the world.* The grapes and the price are the same; the variable this time is the place of origin. Begin with... Sauvignon Blanc from Chile, the Loire Valley, New Zealand, and South Africa.

Producer/Retailer – *some wines are more equal than others.*
Nominally the same type of wine, but which producer makes the finest Italian Chardonnay? Which retailer has the best own-label Rioja? Begin with: Argentinian Malbec.

26 | three steps to heaven
how to taste (and spit) like a pro

The stare-sniff-slurp-swallow-stop guide to tasting wine.

Staring. Apart from being able to spot any floaters, you can tell a little about a wine just by looking at it.

Age. Younger reds tend to be bright purple or ruby, while older ones may be fading to brown. Younger whites are paler than their more golden older relatives.

Concentration. In general, the more concentrated the flavour, the deeper the colour. However, some grape varieties just have more colour than others.

> Young Shiraz and Malbec can be almost inky-black, while Pinot Noir and Nebbiolo fall into the "pale and interesting" category.

Alcoholic strength. When you swirl your glass around (that's why we only fill it a third to half full), how quickly do the last drops of wines (called "tears" or "legs") fall to the bottom? The slower they fall, the stronger the wine.

Sniffing. Vitally important, as the majority of taste receptors are actually in our noses rather than in our mouths. Give your glass a swirl and then take a good sniff. What can you

smell (more of this in Chapter 27)? If you can't smell anything, give the glass another swirl and try again. And if there's still nothing there, don't worry.

> Some wines **leap out of the glass**, others **need coaxing**, while others **never smell like anything much** in the first place.

Slurping. Take a reasonable mouthful, but don't swallow straightaway. Your tongue has taste-buds all over it, so swirl the wine around your mouth and give every bud a chance to react.

```
        Try opening your mouth and breathing
           in some air - you'll look a little
               like an idiot, but it will help
               release more flavours and aromas.
```

And as well as the flavours, think about how the wine feels in your mouth – smooth or rough? Is there a burning sensation that could indicate excessive alcohol?

Swallowing or Spitting. The alcohol may warm your insides, but otherwise what you do is up to you (unless you're in a restaurant, or at a wedding). You'll get the same amount of sensory pleasure either way.

```
            If you want to practise spitting,
               lie in the bathtub and aim for
                                         the taps.
```

When you stop getting complaints from the people in the downstairs apartment, you've mastered it. And finally...

Stopping. How long after you've swallowed or spat can you still taste the wine? How intense is the "finish", as wine folk say? The longer and more intense, the better the wine.

27 | write on

or, tasting notes – why bother?

You don't have to be a wine writer to write something about wine. The internet is full of amateur scribes who would like to be the next Robert Parker or Jancis Robinson (the Brad and Nicole – no: Morgan Freeman and Meryl Streep of the wine-writing world, in case you didn't know). While the message to most is, "Don't give up the day job," these guys and gals obviously get a big thrill from sharing their opinions on wines.

Even if you don't feel like sharing your thoughts on wines with others, writing tasting notes helps you to focus on that important question, "What do I like about this wine?" So dive into that glass. Have a sniff and write down what you think, have a sip and do the same, and then think about the "finish" (*see* previous chapter). For each, write down the first thing that comes into your head. It may be bizarre – I've seen someone write, "Smells like a cushion on which an incontinent person has been sitting" – or it might be quite ordinary: apples, lemons, blackberries, and so on.

> But our memory bank of flavours and aromas is incredibly well-stocked, and it's amazing how many wines ring particular smell-bells that haven't been rung for years.

You might want to look at the back of the bottle to see if the producer has put his own description on the back. Don't be alarmed if it bears no resemblance to what you've written – some of today's best fiction appears on the back of certain bottles. But do have another sip and see if you can detect what the producer did.

When you've written notes on a few wines, take a look at them again and see if you tend to prefer certain styles, countries or grape varieties. Does your description help you remember what the wine was like, or is there something else you think you should have written? Would it have helped you to give the wine a score out of twenty, one hundred or whatever? Are there certain phrases you keep using that you could abbreviate?

> I often put **CFDN** – "**crisp, fresh, dry, neutral**" – for **boring white wines**, for example. A friend of mine uses **AE** for wines he **doesn't** like: "**auto-eject**".

If you really get bitten by the wine bug, you'll soon have a sizeable bank of tasting notes. "Why am I keeping them?" you ask. "When will I ever look at them again?" I might ask the same about those back copies of *Quad Bike Quarterly* that are lurking in your attic. You may revisit your notes, you may not. You decide.

28 | blind-man's bluff
why blind tastings are important

Okay, so you've got the bottles lined up: three wines, including that bargain Cabernet that tasted like it should be double its price. No wonder you dropped in for more last time you passed the shop. You taste all three and – whaddaya know? – your favourite is the Cab. You weren't biased at all, were you?

A look at the label can have an amazing positive and negative influence on our opinion of a wine. It might be that we've never tried the wine before, just that we've had another from the same producer, region, or grape variety in the past – or even the very distant past. Chardonnay-drinkers will often go for any wine that says Chardonnay on the label, regardless of how bad it is. Similarly, give many people a glass of German wine and they'll automatically pour it in the nearest plant pot.

This is why, if you want to get serious about tasting, you should aim to do it "blind". Not blindfolded, not blind-drunk, just "blind". This means that the people doing the spitting don't know what they're tasting, which means they have to keep an open mind about wine. How do you conceal the identities? The best way is to get someone else to pour you a separate glass of each wine (make sure they remember what each one is). If there's no one around, you could number each wine, and then put a small sticker bearing that number on the underside of the glass. Mix them up and you won't know which is which. Otherwise, stick the bottles in bags with ties around their necks, swap them around and start tasting. And take notes – it really helps.

That Cab might come out on top in the blind tasting, but it might not. If it doesn't, maybe it was having an off-day, maybe the bottle wasn't good (*see* Chapter 22), or maybe the other wines were just better. If your blind tastings tell you that you prefer Pinot Noir to Cabernet when you thought the opposite, shouldn't you sit up and take notice?

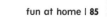

29 | the difference between tasting and drinking

wines to entertain or keep you company

The tasting is over, and there are three bottles (maybe more) with not much missing from them for you and your friends to glug with your dinner, lunch, or even breakfast. (What you do in the safety and comfort of your own home is entirely up to you.)

> So which wine do you choose first?
> The one that tasted best, obviously.

However, halfway through your first glass, it begins to fade, and you wonder whether another of the wines might not have been a better choice. What has happened? Has the wine suddenly changed? No, but the circumstances have. The simple truth – and pardon my English – is that wines that taste good don't necessarily drink good.

Hark back to Chapter 16 about wine shows, and you'll see that even tasters with years of experience can be seduced by bold, full-flavoured wines. But put some (only some, mind you) of these wines with a meal and they can be just too much of a good thing. The oak pokes out like J-Lo's derrière, the ultra-ripe fruit overwhelms any subtlety in the food, while the alcohol leaves a burning sensation in your mouth. Never mind finishing off the bottle – a single glass is a struggle.

> Such wines come from the silicon-
> implant school that says bigger is
> better. With monster trucks and
> professional wrestlers, this may be
> true. With wine, it isn't.

You'll find that the more you get into wine, the less you want to be assaulted by it, and the more you want it to keep you company over the course of a long evening. So when you taste, do so with drinkability in mind. A wine might taste great by itself, but if the bottle's still half-full at the end of the meal, it hasn't done its job.

And while on the subject of wine and wrestling, the first issue of the UK magazine *What Wine?* (now *Wine International*) invited some minor celebrities to take part in a tasting. Among these was a wrestler by the name of Mick McManus, a man known for his figure-four headlocks, but not his literary prowess. Mick's tasting notes were on the sparse side, but the 1980 Robert Mondavi Chardonnay made an impression on him. "Suits my taste," he wrote. Unfortunately, gremlins at the printers caused the great man's words to be modified, and the "u" in suits became an "h"…

30 | mix & match
why not try blending some wine?

Bordeaux, Châteauneuf-du-Pape, Chianti, Rioja, Champagne, port: all European wines, but what else do they have in common? Simply this: all can be made from just one grape variety, but in practice, most are blends in which maybe three, maybe five, maybe – in the case of some – specifically Châteauneuf-du-Pape – thirteen grape varieties are used. True, one particular grape may dominate:

> Chianti is mostly Sangiovese, while Rioja is mostly Tempranillo, for example – but it usually has other varieties in support.

Why? Why, if Grenache is the best grape in Châteauneuf-du-Pape (and it is), do producers not just make a wine that is 100 per cent Grenache? Let's talk steak. If you're planning a steak dinner, then the main event is the slab of meat – big, juicy, cooked to your liking, and sitting there saying, "Eat me." But what if it was just the steak and nothing else? No onions, no red wine sauce... not even any salt. Just a bit primitive?

And never mind just steak, what about beef in general? sizzling steak in black bean sauce. Spaghetti Bolognese.

Chilli con carne. Beef may be the main ingredient, but it's only one part of the dish. So it is with wine.

Some grapes – **Riesling** and **Pinot Noir** spring to mind – are at their best performing **solo**, but many others benefit from having **a little** or **a lot** of something else in the **blend**.

Regulations in some countries allow a wine labelled "Cabernet Sauvignon" to have up to twenty-five per cent of other grapes in the blend, and many producers take full advantage of this opportunity.

There's nothing to stop you doing some experiments with blending at home. All you need is two or more bottles of wine and a spirit of adventure.

Let's say you have a bottle of Chardonnay and one of Sauvignon Blanc. Mixing them in different proportions produces very different results.

Do you want a ripe, peachy Chardonnay that's been given a lift by a small dose of the more aromatic Sauvignon? Or do you want a refreshing, pungent Sauvignon that's been fattened up by a splash of plumper Chardonnay?

And how about Cabernet Sauvignon and Zinfandel? A touch of Zin irons out the gawky edges of the Cabernet.

Conversely, a dose of Cabernet brings some backbone to the otherwise laid-back Zinfandel.

Blending wines is a major part of a winemaker's life, and hopefully he or she will have bottled what they think is the very best blend.

> But if you reckon you can improve a so-so wine by adding a splash of something else, don't think you're committing wine murder.

31 | terms of endearment
words and phrases to impress

"Wet dogs"; "pencil lead"; "strawberry ice-cream". You don't have to spend years tasting wines to come up with descriptions. However, if you want people to think you're in the know, try dropping the following into the conversation.

American oak. As opposed to French oak. A wine aged in an American oak barrel tends to have sweeter, coarser, more vanilla-ish flavours than one that has been in French oak.

Bâtonnage. Remember the sludge (lees) produced during fermentation? *Bâtonnage* is sticking a big paddle or similar device into a vat of wine and stirring the lees. Oatmeal flavours are often a sign of enthusiastic *bâtonnage*.

Botrytis. A fungus that develops in humid conditions, shrivelling the grapes, and concentrating their sugar levels. The grapes look like a write-off, but they can make some of the world's finest sweet wines. A small quantity of botrytized grapes in a dry wine can also add extra interest. Look for flavours of dried apricots and pineapple chunks.

Chaptalization. The addition of sugar to grapes to boost the alcohol level. Carefully done, you shouldn't notice it. However, if a wine tastes "hot" (it burns your mouth) while the flavours are thin, it could have been over chaptalized.

High toast. Another barrel-related term. When barrels are made, they're heated over an open fire in order to bend the staves. Once in shape, the barrel may be further "toasted" to give certain flavours; the longer the toasting, the more pronounced the flavours – of, er, toast.

Malolactic. Which we came across earlier in the book. Should give a buttery richness to a wine, but if badly handled, the butter turns rancid, even cheesy.

pH. Chemistry students will know what this is. Roughly speaking, it's a measure of how much acidity there is in a wine. The higher the pH, the lower the acidity and vice versa. Most wines fall into the 2.9 to 3.5 pH range.

Residual sugar. Any unfermented sugar left after fermentation has either petered out or been halted by the winemaker. Sweet wines obviously have loads, but R.S. is often used to paper over the cracks in many cheaper and supposedly "dry" wines. Just think Mary Poppins and her spoonful of sugar…

Skin contact. Leaving juice from white grapes in contact with their skins for maybe four to twelve hours before fermentation. Well-used, it gives cheaper wines more flavour and texture. Overdone, and you'll find bitter notes like orange or lemon pith.

TCA. Or 2, 4, 6-trichloranisole. This is the musty, mushroomy substance you smell if a wine is "corked", although TCA can arise from sources other than cork.

32-38

under
ground

how to set up your own wine cellar

over
ground

32 | Keeping wine
why bother?

Wine is among the most unusual of foodstuffs. Reams and reams are written about cheese, meat, and vegetables, but only with wine does the concept of "keep-ability" rear its head. When did you last hear of someone having a bacon cellar? When did you last hear of someone laying down a good carrot? (No smutty jokes, please…)

So… let's talk about wine cellars. No, no: come back! The word "cellar" doesn't mean that you need to live in a mansion where the vast, vaulted-ceilinged basement has storage for case upon case of good old claret.

> A **wine cellar** can be a **space under the stairs,** a **box** in the **garage,** and or even a **suitcase under the bed.**

And the reason to have one isn't so you can lay down several dozen bottles of wine for your grandchildren (although they probably wouldn't complain if you did). It's there to provide what you want to drink when you want to drink it.

> All but a tiny proportion of wines are ready to drink the moment they're put on sale. But that's not to say that they'll be at their best on release.

There's no precise definition of what the "best" time is to drink burgundy, or Chianti, or Merlot.

Some people **like their wines** when they are **young and exuberant**, while **others go for them** when they're more **mature and mellow.**

Unless you've tried both, how are you supposed to know which you prefer? And what if you enjoy both? Time was when wine merchants had both the space and the wherewithal to stock several vintages of certain wines.

That time has passed, and it's a rare shop that will have more than just current releases. And when you do find such a merchant, chances are that the older vintages will only be of expensive wines – which is fine if you can afford them, but few can.

Today, if you want to drink older wines regularly, you're either going to have to pay someone to store them for you (and some shops do offer such a service) or do it yourself.

That's the "Why" of wine cellars. For the "How", "What", and "When", read on.

33 | the DIY wine cellar
where and how to keep wine at home

Even those with a purpose-built underground cellar run into problems where wine storage is concerned. Maybe once it was perfect, but now it houses the central heating/the ping-pong table/the grandmother. Fear not. All you need is someplace where the conditions of an old-fashioned cellar can be replicated.

> Wine likes somewhere dark, slightly humid, free of vibrations, and with cool, reasonably constant temperatures.

This immediately rules out that purpose-built rack next to the kitchen stove – unless you want your wine to turn into Madeira. It also means that storing bottles in the bathroom is a no-no. Attics? No: boiling in summer, freezing in winter. But what about that space under the stairs? Or that old fireplace in the guest room? Or a shelf in the bedroom wardrobe? Or even under the bed in a suitcase? With a little ingenuity (and maybe a few polystyrene tiles for insulation), you shouldn't have a problem finding space for a few dozen bottles in even the pokiest of abodes.

Garages and other kinds of outbuildings seem perfect, but just one word of warning. I know someone who had several cases of rather expensive wine that he stored in a friend's wonderful, purpose-built cellar. The friend got divorced and moved to a new house without a cellar. It did, however, have an old railway carriage in the grounds in which there was lots of straw for insulation. Perfect for wine? Not quite. That winter was one of the coldest for many years.

Have you ever put a bottle of wine in the freezer to cool it rapidly and then forgotten about it? The wine freezes and pushes the cork out. Fine, if it's one bottle. But if it's 200 bottles? At around £60/$97 each? But they're still friends. If you're going to use any form of outside storage, keep an eye on that thermometer.

As to how the **bottles** are **stored**, put them on **their sides** to keep the **corks moist**.

There are plenty of purpose-built wine racks around, but these aren't essential. In enclosed areas such as fireplaces, lengths of drainpipe provide suitable cubbyholes for bottles. And there's nothing to stop you from keeping wines in the cardboard cases they came in, although very humid conditions can eventually cause these to collapse.

Finally, if your do-it-yourself skills are non-existent, and your home is a furnace (or an igloo), there is a solution in the form of purpose-built, climate-controlled cabinets that can hold anything up to 300 bottles of wine in ideal conditions. It's just a shame that they cost an arm, a leg, and a major part of the torso…

34 | what's in store?

suggestions for an inexpensive cellar

You don't have to spend megabucks on the wines you put in your cellar. While there's little in the lowest price bracket worth considering, there is plenty for not very much more money. Here are a dozen ideas for candidates for a start-up cellar. Feel free to chop and change, mix and match, or ignore completely.

Red

Côtes du Rhône-Villages. Villages wines are usually a big leap in quality above basic Côtes du Rhône, and cost not too much more. Friendly, herby, and Grenache-based.

Languedoc reds. Once-sleepy southern France is now a hotbed of wine activity. The rich, fruity, and aromatic reds made from Syrah, Grenache, Mourvèdre, and other grapes are great value. The Coteaux du Languedoc is an especially happy hunting ground, with those from the Pic St-Loup enclave being among the finest.

Montsant. Where? An up-and-coming corner of northeastern Spain producing warm, spicy wines from ancient vines. Look for ones from the Capçanes cooperative.

Chilean Cabernet. Save the entry-level wines for everyday glugging and go for the reserve bottlings for the cellar. Juicy essence of cassis usually kissed with oak, tasty on release, but better with a year or two more in bottle.

Australian Shiraz. Again, bypass the cheaper ones, which can be on the jammy side. Some folk will like them in their vibrant, berry-fresh youth. Others, however, will prefer the leathery, meaty notes that a couple of years in the cellar bring.
Argentinian Malbec. As with Shiraz, this drinks well both young and old, providing you're a step above the cheapies. Age brings more mellow, spicy notes to the fragrant cassis and blackberry fruit.

White

New Zealand Riesling. Or, indeed, Riesling from anywhere – most age very well. New Zealand versions have both the zesty, citrus-fruit flavours and floral, aromatic edge of good Riesling, and are usually pretty reliable.
Australian Semillon. With or without oak, this is a wine that needs time to show its true colours. Most blossom from about age three onwards, and some can remain in fine fettle until twenty-plus. Underrated, and thus good value.
White burgundy. And Chablis in particular. Most Chardonnays don't age, but decent white burgundy, that becomes nutty and rich with age, is an exception. Caution: try before you buy.
Sweet Loire Chenin Blanc. Again, try before you buy. But the good wines from Coteaux du Layon and Vouvray are lively and apple-y in their youth, yet age to honeyed splendour.
Non-vintage Champagne. With age Champagne gets richer and toastier. Even basic brands are worth keeping for a year.
Traditional Late-bottled vintage (LBV) port. Vintage port has all the ageing potential. LBV is its more precocious relative, but wines labelled traditional will still evolve in bottle.

35 | in the balance

how to spot a cellar-worthy wine

In wine, the Four Ageing Components of the Apocalypse are acidity, tannin, sweetness, and alcohol.

Acidity. "Yuck," you say. "I don't want my wine to taste acidic." Neither do I. But lemon juice is acidic. I might not want to drink a glassful of lemon juice, but I do enjoy what a little of it does to seafood or a bloody Mary.

Acidity is what makes a wine refreshing.

It also acts as protection against bacteria. Without enough acidity, a wine will taste flat and lifeless, especially as it ages.

Tannin. Another preservative. Tannin is that bitter, butt-clenching substance you taste when you take a mouthful of too-strong tea. In wine, tannins come mainly from grapeskins and seeds, so red wines (where fermentation occurs on the skins; *see* Chapter 10) have more tannin than whites.

Tannins start off as small chains of molecules, but these join together and eventually precipitate as the wine ages – hence the sediment in older bottles.

The longer the chains, the smoother the wine's texture; that's why a rough, young red can become a silky, mature beauty.

Sweetness. Any jam-makers out there? What do you add to the fruit to preserve it? Right: sugar. Sugar by itself makes a gloopy, cloying wine. It needs something to balance it, so it's back to that lemon juice again. In sweet wines, sugar and acidity are like the two ends of a seesaw. If the balance is right, you're thrilled. If it's not, then no one is happy.

Alcohol. Just think of peaches in brandy.

```
Yet there's more to an age-worthy
        wine than acidity, tannin,
        sweetness, and/or alcohol.
```

These four substances can be thought of as the bones of a wine. If there's just not enough flesh – flavour, in other words – hanging on them, or if the flesh tastes downright awful, then no amount of time in bottle is going to make a difference.

But if the flavour seems to be in balance with the bones, AND YOU LIKE THE FLAVOUR (some people forget that important point), then the wine is a candidate for keeping. You'll get some wines wrong. Every person who's ever kept wine has been left with some dogs.

```
But the more you experiment, the
        fewer will be your bottles of
                the canine variety.
```

36 | the age of reason

why wine is better too young than too old

"I have five bottles of 1977 Beaujolais that have been sitting around since 1979. I was wondering what to do with them."

> Every wine hack has encountered at least one Monty Python-esque character (almost invariably male) who accosts them when they least expect it with such a statement.

Being restrained folk, we resist the desire to tell them in precise anatomical detail what they should do with these dinosaurs of wine and mutter something vague like, "Oh really?"

The line of questioning then usually takes one of two turns. 1. "How much are they worth?" The correct answer to this is, "Does the term 'negative equity' mean anything to you?" *Or* 2. "When should I drink them?" The sad truth is that even the medical skills of the impossibly glamorous doctors on *ER* would have no effect on this wine. For several years, it has been in the grave.

> Those born in 1977 might be interested in the bottles as curios, but as for drinking the contents — forget it.

How long you should keep a wine depends on a couple of things. First, there's the wine itself. The Beaujolais may be long gone, but not all wines from 1977 will be in such a dodo-like state. For example, it's a great vintage for port.

Similarly, a **ten-year-old New Zealand Sauvignon** is probably **too old**, while a **ten-year-old** high-class **California Cabernet Sauvignon** will still be **up for it.**

But secondly, and just as importantly, there's your taste in wines. Take that California Cabernet. If you like exuberant, fruity wines, maybe you should have drunk it five years earlier. If you prefer them supple and mellow, then you might want to keep it for five more years. If you're not sure whether a wine is on the way up or down, try this simple test.

```
If the last glass from the bottle
       tastes better than the first,
  then it's still improving. If it
doesn't, then any other bottles need
              polishing off soon.
```

Whatever you do, don't keep it "just in case". There are countless bottles of wine around the world slumbering in people's basements, garages, and closets that are just deteriorating by the day. A total waste. Someone once said,

> "Appreciating old wine is like making love to a very old lady. It is possible; it can even be enjoyable. But it requires a bit of imagination."

So if in doubt, pull out the corks sooner rather than later. You may find a slightly awkward teenager, but isn't that better than finding a corpse?

37 | vintage chart, vintage schmart

beware the numbers game

I think I've said it before, but I'll say it again. Wine is made from *grapes* (but you knew that anyway). Now, grapes are an agricultural product, and thus are subject to the vagaries of the weather. In some regions, the weather is fairly predictable, and those growing the grapes don't need to sit with their ears glued to the weather forecast. In other regions, the weather is fickle. One year will be brilliantly sunny and dry, the next dismal and dull. Good years, bad years, and so-so years.

Yet when you ask a winemaker to describe the last few vintages, you often get an answer something like this:

> "Nineteen ninety-five was very good, so were '96, '98, and 2000; '97 and 2001 were good; '99 average to good; and 2002 was average." So when was the last below-average vintage? "Hmm, we haven't had one of those for a long time; '93 maybe?"

Those who are pedantic about the semantic will be shuddering at this abuse of the word "average". Let 'em. Our winemaker isn't there for his linguistic skills; he's there to make the best wine he can, whatever nature throws at him.

Which brings me on to vintage charts: those tables that give a rating for the wines of a particular region in a particular year. Sounds like a useful thing to have? Ish.

Faced with two bottles of Château Blob Chardonnay, one from 2002 and one from 2001, a quick look at the vintage chart would show you that 2002 was a much better year. But what the vintage chart doesn't tell you is that Château Blob 2002 isn't as good as the 2001 from its neighbour, Domaine Bucket.

It also **doesn't tell you** that **good producers** can make **good wine** in **bad vintages.**

Hence our winemaker's struggle to recall something that was "below-average".The message, then, is not to get hung up on vintage charts; it's much more useful to know your Bucket from your Blob.

Once you've settled on a group of good, reliable producers, by all means commit a few vintage ratings to mind, but don't let them dominate your buying decisions. Those setting up cellars often get sucked in by wine sellers' hype – "A 'Must-Buy' vintage", "Vintage of the Century", and so on – and buy far too much at one whack.

That 2000 Bordeaux might be fabulous, but do you really want to drink nothing else for the next ten years?

38 | the ancient order of bottle-fondlers

wine is for drinking, not worshipping

A friend of mine was on a plane to New York, and found himself sitting next to a boisterous Californian. After a while it came out that my friend was a wine writer.

"Oh, really?" said the American. "Well, I'm a wine collector."

Friend: "And what exactly does that involve?"

American: "Oh, I guess it means that I buy more wine than I actually drink."

Friend: "In that case, I'm really pleased to meet you. You see, I have the opposite problem…"

End of conversation.

There is something rather pleasing about an array of silent green bottles in a well-stocked cellar (especially with a cobweb or two to add atmosphere), and there are some people who treat theirs like monastic retreats, as places to escape from the hubbub of the world. But buying more than you are going to drink? I mean, honestly, what is the point? I call it Pinot Envy. There are some people for whom wine is not a drink but a chance for one-upmanship. They will proudly show off their extensive collection to all and sundry, and might even let them fondle some of the more desirable bottles (and magnums – these folk *love* magnums). But come mealtime, what are the visitors offered? Something cheap and not particularly cheerful.

Wine is a food product. It's meant to be drunk, not collected as if it were porcelain thimbles. Can you imagine someone proudly showing off their collection of sausages?

Don't become a hoarder, buying wine that you're never going to have time to drink. If your cellar is getting crowded, just invite some friends over to help you polish off the excess. And if you do give the bottles a little stroke, I won't tell anyone.

how to show wines at their best

serving
for the
match

39 | the heat is on

don't get hung up on serving temperatures

I have in front of me a bottle of wine made from Tannat. The traditional home of this chunky grape variety is southwest France, where it is responsible for the chewy reds of Madiran. This particular example, however, hails from Uruguay. The back label says, "Serve at room temperature." Hmm. Now which "room" would that be? My office in the north of England? Maybe a room in southwest France? Or perhaps one in Uruguay?

Traditional wisdom has it that red wine should be served at "room temperature". However, the origins of this traditional wisdom lie in pre-central-heating days, when gentlemen wore several layers of woollens beneath their frock coats.

> The temperature of rooms then would be unbearably low for wimpy 21st-centurions, but it was pretty good for serving a red wine.

It was warm enough so that the wine's bitter tannins didn't poke out, but cool enough for the fruit to remain refreshing. Cut to today, when our living rooms are so many degrees warmer than those of 150 years ago. The hike in room temperature has not been kind to wine.

The alcohol jumps out of the glass, obliterating any subtlety and muddying the flavours. Room temperature it may be, but it certainly doesn't make for a quality drinking experience.

There's also a bottle of South African white wine on my desk. This one says "Serve well-chilled" – I'm presuming it means the wine rather than me. I'm always suspicious of wines that say "serve well-chilled"; it's all to do with ice-cream. Straight from the freezer (OK, maybe with a quarter of an hour to acclimatize), ice-cream tastes great. But leave a sludgy dose in the bottom of your bowl, and what happens? It melts. Warm ice-cream is *not* nice: fatty, sweet, crude in flavour.

Back to wine. If a wine says that it should be drunk as cold as possible, then it usually means that at warmer temperatures, like our ice-cream, it tastes foul. But just imagine if it was a decent white wine. Chilled to death, it just tastes cold and wet. A slightly warmer temperature is actually kind to the wine, bringing out the extra flavours for which you've paid a premium.

The bottom line is this:

> Most **red wine** is served **too warm**, **most white wine** is served **too cold.**

So don't put that Chardonnay in to chill a week before you're going to open it – an hour or so will be fine. And don't put that Merlot on top of the oven – fifteen minutes in the fridge might be just what it needs, too.

40 | doing the decant thing

why you sometimes need to let wine breathe

Forget those images of crusty butlers in crusty pantries.

> There's nothing snobbish about a
> practice that makes wine more
> pleasurable.

I'm talking, of course, about decanting wine. There are two reasons for decanting.

The first is sludge. Given time, most red wines will throw a deposit made up of tannins, tartrate crystals, and colouring pigments. You won't come to any harm drinking (eating?) this, but it doesn't look very nice in the glass.

> Quite how much **sludge** there is depends on the **age** and **type** of the **wine.**

Vintage port is full of it; Pinot Noir (even when old) hardly has any. You can often tell by holding the bottles up to the light.

The second reason is because it makes a wine taste better. Some wines are just plain awkward, and need a little persuasion to show their true colours. Others are just too boisterous and need time to calm down.

With good, young wine especially,
it's a rare bottle that doesn't
benefit from a couple of hours
of what, in winespeak, is called
"breathing".

And "breathing" always means decanting. There's no point
in just removing the cork and letting the bottle stand there.
That's not breathing; that's sitting there with an open mouth.

As for how to decant, there are convoluted decanting
cradles that you can buy, where you turn a handle to tilt the
bottle so the wine dribbles out slowly and gently without
disturbing the sediment. The words "sledgehammer",
"crack", and "nut" spring to mind. Leave these for those
with more money than sense.

Nor is it necessary to have ornate
decanters (although these do look kind
of pretty when full of fine red wine).
All you need is a glass jug and a
steady hand.

In fact, if it's a young wine you're dealing with, you
don't even need the steady hand, as there shouldn't be
much sediment. Simply tip it into the jug/decanter, and
then leave it until you're ready to drink it.

A little more care is needed with older wines. If you
pour out the wine slowly, you should be able to see when
the first wisps of sediment appear. Stop at that point and
use what's left in the gravy.

It's not just **red wines** that need **decanting**. **Whites** don't produce much **sediment**, but they can be just as prone to **sulkiness** as reds.

But if you do decide to decant them, you may want to pour them back into the bottle afterwards; having something that looks like a urine sample sitting on the dinner table can take away your appetite.

41 | give & you shall receive
don't be mean with your merlot

Get into wine and sooner or later you'll come up against a dilemma. It's this: some good friends/close relatives are coming over for dinner and they really, *really* don't know anything about wine, apart from that it's red, white, and pink and "does the biz". You've gone to town on the food, but when it comes to the wine… well, wouldn't they be happy with any old sludge? Perhaps you could stash a bottle of something nice in the kitchen and keep going in for a top-up while the rest of the table sips Bargain-Bin Blanc.

Stop a moment and think of your CD collection. Do you look at some of the music and think, "I'm not playing that; they wouldn't appreciate it"? Or your wardrobe. Are some of the clothes just too exclusive for your guests? No, and you shouldn't adopt a similar mind-set with wine. At some point, someone poured you a wine that made you think, "Wow! This transcends the boundaries of fermented grape juice. It boldly goes where no wine has gone before."Or words to that effect. Did they look at you and think "Wine virgin"? No. They shared what they had with a non-believer, and you were converted.

I'm not saying that you should crack open your finest bottles for all and sundry, just that you should aim to take them a step or two beyond what they're used to. So if bargain basement is their norm, try them with a mid-priced wine. And don't introduce it with any fanfare, giving details of all but the name of the winemaker's pet ferret. People who are into wine often make the mistake of thinking the whole subject is of universal interest – it isn't. So put the bottle on the table and let everyone enjoy it, politely ignoring those who add a large splash of soda to their glasses.

42 | ice-cream and claret
experiment with food and wine

Psst! Quick, while no one's looking: I have a confession to make. My publisher has a great catalogue of wine books, but among them there are some that relate to food and wine matching. I'll come clean. My attitude to the subject is best summed up by the statement, "Food and Wine Matching: Art, Science, or Bull****?"

Don't get me wrong; there are some food and wine marriages that are made in heaven, and others made in hell, but these are few and far between. Most fall halfway between these two extremes. Moreover, put five wines and five dishes in front of five people and ask them which wines work best, and the lack of consensus will be deafening.

Here are my own five fairly brief "rules" on food and wine matching.

1. Loud wine, quiet food; quiet wine, loud food. The stronger and more diverse the flavours in a dish, the more they'll fight with a powerful wine, so pick a simple one –

> ### Pinot Grigio for white and Beaujolais for red are two of my favourites.

Conversely, if you want to show the wine off, have a simple meal: plain roast chicken works well with both whites and reds.

2. Acid casualty. That Muscadet that seems kind of tart by itself is suddenly lively and refreshing with a plate of food. Conversely, that rather lush, peachy Chardonnay that tasted great on the patio has turned into a bimbo over dinner. It's all because of acidity.

```
Wines without enough acidity fall flat
                             with food.
```

3. When in Rome... drink as the Romans do. In other words, if you're having a dish that is associated with a particular region/country, try to find the local wines.

4. Take that wine away from my cheese. Red wine and cheese? If the wine is mellow and the cheese is hard, then maybe. But I often find white wine of whatever sweetness a much better bet with a selection of cheeses.

5. Breaking and entering. Break any rules you know. Like red wine with red meat, white wine with white meat and fish. And the four rules before this one. Experiment, and if it tastes good to you, then do it. My grandpa-in-law drank sweet wine all through the meal, and he always had a smile on his face.

And that's it. I would struggle to expand these to fill a book. If you find a great food and wine match, then hooray for you. If you find a foul one, then have a piece of bread, a swig of water, and move on.

43 | making a meal of it

**why not all restaurants are wine-lovers'
friends, how to spot the good one, plus BYO**

"And before your very eyes, the Great Restaurato will
transform a dirt-cheap bottle of wine into an outrageously
overpriced one!" I'm not the only person who thinks
that many restaurateurs are taking the Piesporter with the
mark-ups they slap on bottles of wine.

> **The excuse?** The buying, storage,
> service, and dishwashing all cost
> money. True. But they don't cost that
> much money.

Thankfully, there are restaurants that take a more sensible
approach to wine pricing; for wines above a certain price,
they may just add on a flat amount, for example. They reckon
that if someone thinks he's getting the wine at a fair price,
he'll order some more and be more likely to come back.

Other signs of a wine-friendly restaurant? How about the
glasses? If they're big, unadorned, tulip-shaped affairs that
can hold a goodly measure and still be less than half full,
then things are looking up. If they're chipped, ancient
goblets, then brace yourself.

Then there's the wine list. Plenty of wines available by
the glass, and several half-bottles is a good start. Both give
you the chance to either drink sparingly, or maybe enjoy

several different wines with your meal. As for the size of the list? Hmm. A decent list should aim to cover as many styles and prices as possible in the smallest number of wines. There are good lists running to twenty wines, and there are bad ones running to several hundred. If it is a 600-strong list, it'll probably be accompanied by a wine waiter or sommelier.

> A good sommelier is worth his weight in tips. A bad one is worth his weight in cowpats.

Good ones are genuinely helpful and steer you towards the best wines for your price range and choice of food. Bad ones intimidate you with their superior knowledge, and you often end up paying far more than you'd bargained for.

And finally, there's the service. Many restaurants commit the reds-too-warm, whites-too-cold crime. Ask for an ice bucket or even a new bottle for that semi-boiling red. Stop the waiter from plunging that semi-frozen white back into the ice bucket. And at all times, if you don't want your glass to be topped up, just tell the staff to back off – remember, you're paying for the wine.

But you don't always have to. Many restaurants (and especially if you're a regular) can be persuaded to offer BYO – bring your own wine, that is. There'll often be a "corkage" charge for this, particularly in places which already have a decent wine selection, but since this is usually much less than the mark-up you'd have paid for something from the list, you're still much better off.

44-50

smart buys in wine

words of
wisdom

44 | off the beaten track
wines to discover before anyone else does

Looking for life beyond me-too Merlot? Here are a few suggestions to help you expand your drinking horizons.

Argentina. If you've tried the juicy Malbec, move on to the fragrant Bonarda and plummy Barbera. For whites, the gently spicy Torrontés is good summer drinking.

Australia. Despite interest in the quince-like Verdelho, it's regions rather than grape varieties that are all the talk Down Under.

> Up-and-coming places include Pemberton, Frankland River, Limestone Coast, and Orange.

Austria. Classic dry wines from Riesling and Grüner Veltliner – white pepper, grapefruit, lentils – plus sumptuous sweet wines. Reds are coming along in leaps and bounds, too.

Chile. Chile's specialty is the soft, herbal-edged Carmenère. Too brassy on its own, it's far better bringing spice and softness to Cabernet Sauvignon and Merlot blends.

France. The reds from the Languedoc-Roussillon and Côtes du Rhône are among the best value in the world.

In more **traditional regions, Mâconnais whites** from **Burgundy, Côtes de Castillon reds** from **Bordeaux,** and **anything from Alsace** are **smart buys.**

Germany. The great estates continue to make great Riesling, both dry and sweet. The novelty is that people outside Germany are now drinking them. Don't miss these fabulous wines.

Italy. Massively exciting, and a total pain to keep up with.

In the **south, local grapes** such as **Negroamaro, Primitivo,** and **Nero d'Avola** are being **put to good use.**

There's plenty of activity on the Tuscan coast, with Sangiovese (the Chianti grape), Cabernet Sauvignon, and Merlot. In the north, look for sexed-up modern Barbera and the weird and wonderful whites of Friuli.

New Zealand. For whites, Pinot Gris is all the rage, especially if it comes from Central Otago. This is also home to terrific but pricey Pinot Noir. Look, too, for Hawke's Bay Syrah.

Portugal. New-wave Portuguese reds combine the freshness of modern wine with the heavily scented tobacco, berry, and plum of Portugal. The Douro (home of port) is the sexy region, Touriga Nacional the in-demand grape.

South Africa. Another place where Syrah is all the rage, and Cape Blends (thirty to seventy per cent Pinotage, plus Cabernet and Merlot) are also on the up. Cape winemakers seemed finally to have mastered Sauvignon Blanc, but don't ignore the upmarket Chenin Blancs.

Spain. Rioja has been revitalized (now there's oak AND fruit), while great Tempranillo is also emerging from Ribera del Duero and Toro.

> Priorato and Montsant are making brilliant, spicy reds. There are even decent wines from the massive La Mancha region.

For whites, Rueda, Rías Baixas, and fino sherry are what you should be seen drinking.

USA. Alternatives to Cabernet are being made by the "Rhône Rangers" (Californians who follow a particular French style). Syrah, Mourvèdre, Grenache, Marsanne, Roussanne, and Viognier are the in-demand grapes.

> There's also the Cal-Ital brigade – Sangiovese, Nebbiolo, Barbera, Refosco, and more.

Further north, Washington State Cabernets and Merlots, and Oregon Pinot Noir and Pinot Gris challenge the Golden State's supremacy.

45 | top of the world

why you should try the classics at least once

It's one o'clock in the morning, and I should have finished this book a month ago. Where do I go for inspiration for the final few chapters? To the classics: a mature, red Bordeaux to be precise. The first glass is a little broody (remember Chapter 40 – "Doing the decant thing"?), the second (it's now 2AM; I've taken time out to play Solitaire) is just hitting its stride, and by the third glass, the muse has returned with a large grin and an even larger box of chocolates. It is, put simply, beautiful wine.

There's quite a leap from good wine to great wine. Good wine lubricates weekends, but great wine… Well, if you're the gabby type, great wine makes you shut up for an instant. If you're the strong but silent type, great wine stimulates your vocal cords. Great wine makes you sit up and take notice.

> However, **great wines** are **rare**, **great wines** are usually **expensive**, and **great wines** are **fickle** – if you get them on an **off-day**, you're in for a **major disappointment**.

But even so, you owe it to yourself to try as many great wines as possible. So what makes a wine great? I call it "life beyond fruit".

There are plenty of "fruity" wines around; in fact, there are many that are just too fruity. But a great wine has far more than just fruit. It should be seamless, meaning that even when it's young, you can't see the joins between the fruit, the oak (if it's been in a barrel), the terroir, the winemaking, and the alcohol. It doesn't actually have to be full-bodied, but it should be full-flavoured, and it should also smell wonderful – just sniffing it should give as much pleasure as actually drinking it.

There are old greats –

Red and white burgundy, dry red and sweet white Bordeaux, red and white Hermitage, vintage port, German Riesling, vintage Champagne, Tokaji from Hungary

– and there are new greats –

Napa Cabernet, South Australian Shiraz Super-Tuscan reds, Austrian Riesling.

Choose where you start exploring greatness, but do it with the help of an understanding wine merchant. Say something like, "My favourite type of wine is X. I've got £50/$75 and I want a wine that blows my socks off." This much for a bottle of wine? Yes. You blow more than that on a good night out, and you'll almost certainly spend more on a serious shopping spree. You don't have to fork out that much every week, just once or twice a year. So start saving. It's worth it.

46 | proceed with caution
the world's most overrated wines

Having waxed lyrical about great wines, I'm now going to wax raucously about mediocre wines. I'm not talking here about cheap and mediocre; I'm thinking of wines at first-class prices that offer a cattle-class experience.

You can try making excuses in such cases: maybe the wine was having a bad-hair day, maybe it was too young/old, maybe it clashed with the food. But the fact remains that the wine didn't deliver the goods. You pushed the boat out and the boat sank.

> No region is immune to these mutton-dressed-as-lamb wines, but some are more populated with them than others.

Often the places that offer some of the greatest wine experiences also have more than their fair share of offenders. Here are five of the worst culprits.

Red burgundy. I once wrote that great burgundy was in some ways like an orgasm: if you're not sure whether you've had one, you haven't, and if you have had one, then you want another as soon as possible. Unfortunately, much of the life of a burgundophile – especially one with a taste for

the reds – consists of unqualified frustration. Standards in Burgundy are improving, but too many wines still lack the "yes, Yes, YES!" factor.

Red Bordeaux. There's too much laurel-sitting-on in the world's largest fine-wine region.

> Several châteaux make classy wine in most vintages, but the pricing policies of many seem to be dictated by what the tea leaves say rather than by economic realities.

For a place with 12,000-plus producers, there simply aren't enough good wines at a decent price.

Rioja. Another large and complacent region. There are old-wave wines that still spend too long in old-oak barrels, losing their fruit on the way.

> There are new-wave wines in expensive, heavy bottles that make you think, "So what?"

Thankfully, there are now also some movers and shakers who are, er, moving and shaking Rioja.

California Cabernet Sauvignon. "And this is a good everyday Cabernet, sensibly priced at $30…" Od's bodkins.

If I were paying $30/£20 for my "everyday" wine, I'd expect to be getting at least a magnum. But the sad truth is that that $30 California Cabernet often does taste like an everyday wine. Clean, fruity, and honest. But too simple.

Champagne. Damn the mystique:

> A lot of **Champagne** is a **rip-off.**

Spain's cava is made in the same way, yet it sells for a fraction of the price. Great Champagne is truly great (and it doesn't have to be too expensive). But there's simply too much of the stuff around that just isn't worth the money.

47 | compare & contrast, part I

if you like that red, you'll probably like this one

Twelve popular red wines, plus suggestions for alternatives.

Australian Shiraz. Instead of the big, meaty ones, try South African Pinotage, California Zinfandel. Instead of the more restrained versions, try Rhône reds such as Crozes-Hermitage and Costières de Nîmes.

Beaujolais. The Gamay grape doesn't crop up much in other parts of the world, but other juicy, light reds can be found, among them Dolcetto from Italy, Loire reds (Bourgueil, Chinon, and Saumur-Champigny), and lighter burgundies.

Bordeaux. Virtually every wine-producing country has wines made from Merlot and Cabernet Sauvignon; New Zealand probably comes closest to Bordeaux in style. And try other wines of South West France such as Cahors, Bergerac, Côtes de Duras, and Côtes du Frontonnais.

Burgundy. Seek out Pinots from New Zealand, Oregon, Sonoma, and Santa Barbara in California, and various parts of the state of Victoria in Australia. Also, Nebbiolo in northern Italy (Barolo and Barbaresco are the big two) offers something of the Burgundian finesse and fragrance.

Cabernet Sauvignon. The king of grapes (Chardonnay is queen) has a close relative called Cabernet Franc that is lighter and leafier (and used for most Loire reds – see Beaujolais, above). Other firm, fruity grapes include Malbec and Portugal's Touriga Nacional.

Chianti/Tuscan Sangiovese. Ranges from pale and wan to firm and full-bodied. Instead of the former, check out Beaujolais. Instead of the latter, look at Bordeaux and Spain's Ribera del Duero.

Chilean Merlot. Which may or may not include a large proportion of a totally different grape called Carmenère. Merlot from elsewhere is seldom so plump and plummy, but Italian wines made from Montepulciano and Barbera can be.

Côtes du Rhône. Like Chianti, hugely variable. The same grapes are used throughout southern France and northeastern Spain (home of Priorat and Montsant). And a step up brings you to the majesty of Châteauneuf-du-Pape and Gigondas.

Port. California, South Africa, and Australia produce their own, often very commendable versions, while Roussillon in France has the figgy-rich Banyuls, Maury, and Rivesaltes. Italy's Recioto isn't fortified, but it is powerful, rich, and sweet.

Rioja. Tempranillo, the grape behind most Rioja, crops up throughout Spain, but Navarra, Ribera del Duero, and Toro are the main challengers in quality terms. Mature Pinot Noir can offer something of the mellow strawberry edge.

Valpolicella. Many reds from northern Italy (Trentino Merlot, Dolcetto, Bardolino, Teroldego) are in the same light, bitter, cherryish vein. Austria's Blauer Zweigelt also comes close.

Zinfandel. Pinotage and Shiraz offer the same bear-hug-in-a-glass of good Zin. Alternatively, why not go back to Zin's roots in southern Italy (where it is called Primitivo) and try the wines made from Negroamaro and Nero d'Avola?

48 | compare & contrast, part II

if you like that white, you'll probably like this one

Twelve popular white (-ish) wines, plus suggestions for alternatives.

Burgundy. Usually 100 per cent Chardonnay, so Chardonnays from other parts of the world are the obvious substitutes. Dry white Bordeaux, made from Sauvignon Blanc and Sémillon, can also achieve similar class.

Champagne. Australia, New Zealand, California, and Spain (upmarket cava) all produce decent, widely available fizz. The sparklers of Franciacorta in Italy and (honestly) England can also deliver the goods.

Chardonnay. For many people, white wine IS Chardonnay – or that from the New World, at least. Australian whites made from Semillon, Verdelho, and Marsanne also deliver a tasty, weighty experience.

Fino sherry. Pretty good, sherry-style wines are to be found in South Africa and Australia, although few are exported. You should be able to track down some dry Montilla – sherry-like in style, although not always fortified.

Italian Pinot Grigio. Pinot Grigio/Gris from other parts of the world seldom has the crispness of Italian versions. Opt instead for other Italian whites like Gavi, Pinot Bianco, and Arneis.

Liebfraumilch. If it's bland and sweet you're after, I'm not going to help you. Much better to lose the Lieb and go for wines made from Riesling – Australia and New Zealand produce the friendliest versions.

Muscadet. Think of wines from places that eat a lot of seafood. How about Portugal's Vinho Verde, the rapidly improving Assyrtiko-based wines from Santorini in Greece, and Spain's Rías Baixas – more flavour but just as fish-friendly?

New Zealand Sauvignon Blanc. South Africa and Australia are finally making good Sauvignon. And do try the wines that first inspired the Kiwis: Sancerre, Pouilly-Fumé, and Menetou-Salon from the Loire Valley.

Sauternes/sweet white Bordeaux. Sauternes isn't as sweet as some sweet wines – the folk in Bordeaux drink it with blue cheese or foie gras rather than desserts. Try equally classy stickies from Austria and Tokaji in Hungary.

Soave. Many Italian whites fall into the slightly neutral and nutty camp. So, too, does unoaked white Rioja. The whites of southern France and the Côtes du Rhône are similar in style, but somewhat richer in flavour.

South African Chenin Blanc. Chenin Blanc from the Loire (Vouvray, Anjou) is totally different. Opt instead for Chenins from California and Australia, or for the equally peachy but far more aromatic Viognier.

White Zinfandel. Varies from frivolous to frightful. Sources of finer but equally welcoming rosés include southern France and Spain (Navarra especially), though few are as sweet as white Zin.

49 | bordeaux boredom
the dangers of becoming a wine geek

Nearly at the end now, and hopefully you'll have mustered some enthusiasm for wine. It is possible, however, to muster a little *too* much, as you'll know if you've ever come across a wine geek. I suppose every topic has its share of obsessives, and at least with wine, the subject of their passion does taste nice. Still, that doesn't make them any less dull.

They're usually easy to spot at parties. While everyone else is intent on having a good time, their brows are furrowed. Rather than just drink whatever wine is available, they're scanning the labels of bottles, checking what percentage of Shiraz or Cabernet each wine contains, and whether the winemaker thinks it is appropriate for the food on offer (although I've never seen a label that suggests a wine to serve with Pringles and pretzels). And they ignore the stack of plastic cups, heading furtively for the kitchen to see if they can track down a more suitable vessel for their chosen libation.

> If you find yourself cornered by a wine geek, whatever you do, don't utter the words, "Well they all taste the same to me."

Not unless you want three hours of one-way traffic about canopy management, micro-oxygenation, and the difference between a *grosslage* and an *einzellage*. You long to say to these people, "Get out more! Drink some beer!"

But now that you know some more about wine, is there a risk that you, too, might be joining the nerd herd?

Ten signs that you might be turning into a wine geek:
1. You make notes on the wines when you're out for dinner.
2. You keep back copies of wine magazines.
3. You have a collection of bottle labels.
4. You have more than one tie with a wine motif.
5. You can recite the 1855 Classification of Bordeaux châteaux.
6. You can name all thirteen grapes in Châteauneuf-du-Pape.
7. You insist on correcting people who mispronounce Riesling – (it's Reece-ling, by the way).
8. You look down your nose at people who drink nothing but Chardonnay.
9. You can't remember your last vacation that wasn't in a wine region.
10. You have more corkscrews than pairs of shoes.

50 | you are still right

Fifty chapters later, you are still right. Your goalposts of "rightness" may have shifted by a large distance, or hardly at all, but that's fine by me. My job is not to force you to like particular wines but just to point and say, "Look, taste, drink".

There are three things in particular I'd encourage you to do. First, taste a little more – it's the quickest and most enjoyable way to learn about wine. A producer once told me that one of his wines tasted of roof-tiles. I didn't believe him – until I tasted it. Second, spend a little more. There's plenty of perfectly competent stuff at the bottom end of the market, but it's amazing how much extra flavour you get by spending a bit extra. And don't forget to treat yourself two or three times a year. Third, talk to your wine merchant a little more. The world's most interesting wines are usually made in quantities far too small for major retailers to consider, which is where the specialists come in. Good merchants offer better wines, better service and better advice.

And as for "I don't know much about wine but I know what I like," is that still you? Whether it is or not, I'd welcome any comments you have on this book, or on wine in general – drop me a note at idontknowmuch@simonwoods.com.

OK, that's it. Now go open a bottle.

Simon Woods, Summer 2003